ABC
NEWSROOM

—

Shigeru Yamane
Kathleen Yamane

2

JN125955

KINSEIDO

Kinseido Publishing Co., Ltd.

3-21 Kanda Jimbo-cho, Chiyoda-ku,
Tokyo 101-0051, Japan

Copyright © 2024 by Shigeru Yamane
Kathleen Yamane

All rights reserved. No part of this publication may be reproduced, stored in a retrieval system, or transmitted, in any form or by any means, electronic, mechanical, photocopying, recording or otherwise, without the prior permission of the publisher.

First published 2024 by Kinseido Publishing Co., Ltd.

Cover design: Haruka Ito
Text design: DAITECH co., ltd.
Editorial support: Aoi Nishida
Video Material: Copyright © 2023 ABC, Inc.

🎧 音声ファイル無料ダウンロード

https://www.kinsei-do.co.jp/download/4190

この教科書で 🎧 DL 00 の表示がある箇所の音声は、上記 URL または QR コードにて無料でダウンロードできます。自習用音声としてご活用ください。

▶ PC からのダウンロードをお勧めします。スマートフォンなどでダウンロードされる場合は、ダウンロード前に「解凍アプリ」をインストールしてください。

▶ URL は、検索ボックスではなくアドレスバー (URL 表示欄) に入力してください。

▶ お使いのネットワーク環境によっては、ダウンロードできない場合があります。

◎ CD 00　左記の表示がある箇所の音声は、教室用 CD (Class Audio CD) に収録されています。

Foreword

World News Tonight, the flagship news program of the American Broadcast Company, is enjoyed by millions of Americans each evening at 6:30. Watching it together was part of my family's daily routine when I was growing up in New York. With its reputation for balanced, fair reporting by a news team who take a personalized look at what's happening around the world, the show is consistently at the top of the evening news ratings.

Since the publication of this textbook series began more than three decades ago, the popular newscasts have become part of the learning experience of tens of thousands of Japanese students, as well. This text is the second in our new series, incorporating a number of changes to enhance the learning experience. As always, we have made every effort to select stories that are not only important but will also make young adults think a little bit harder about the world outside of Japan. This edition includes a stimulating cross section of topics, from ChatGPT technology to the student loan controversy and the challenge of accessing clean water. You will meet inspiring heroes like the high school students who created a prosthesis for their teacher's dog; a 12-year old boy whose Toy Project provides Christmas gifts to children with cancer; and Sister Jean, the beloved 103-year-old chaplain of a college basketball team. These news stories will take you all across the U.S. and beyond, to glimpse the effects of climate change in New Zealand and witness the heated protests over pension reform in France. We feel certain that you will find them all to be as fascinating as we do.

Back in 1987, no one associated with this ABC World News textbook project imagined that the series would have such longevity and touch the lives of so many students. We believe that adopting authentic broadcast news materials for classroom use is a powerful way to build English skills while also helping students to become more knowledgeable about world affairs and to develop the critical thinking skills necessary for all young people in today's increasingly interconnected world. Many of our students also tell us that using the text was good preparation for the TOEFL and TOEIC exams and for job interviews.

To the students using *ABC NEWSROOM*, remember that the skills that you develop using this book can be applied to other news shows, even when the course is over. We sincerely hope that you will challenge yourselves to become more aware of world events and be inspired to follow the news more closely. Happy studying!

January, 2024

Kathleen Yamane
Shigeru Yamane

まえがき

日常生活における情報源として，インターネットが年代を問わず欠かせないツールとなっている。このような高度な情報化社会では，不正確な情報や見方の偏った情報も多くあふれている。学生諸君は，何が本当に自分に役立つ正しい情報か，情報の「質」を見極める能力を身につける必要があるのではないだろうか。

一般的に，テレビニュースからの情報は信頼性が高いといわれている。本書はアメリカの3大ネットワーク（ABC，CBS，NBC）の一つである，ABC放送からのテレビニュースを文字化した上で，テキスト用に編集したものである。収録したニュースは米国東部標準時間夕方6時30分から毎日放送されているABC放送の看板ニュース番組 *ABC World News Tonight with David Muir* である。

1948年に始まり，長い歴史を誇るこのABC放送のニュース番組は，ピーター・ジェニングズなど，多くの人気キャスターを生み出してきた。2014年にディビッド・ミューアがアンカーパーソンに抜擢され，さらに人気が高まった。2015年3月には「アメリカで最も多く視聴されている夕方のニュース番組」となり，アメリカ国内でも絶大な人気を保ちながら，質の高い情報を毎日提供し続けている。

今回も，そのABC放送の看板番組の中から，大学生が学ぶにふさわしい多種多様なニュースを15本厳選し，収録することができた。「学生ローンの返済が免除へ」，「画期的な結婚尊重法が成立」など，本書で取り上げた現代社会が抱えるさまざまなトピックを学ぶことを通じて，学生諸君にはニュースの理解を深めながら，自分の意見も持ってもらいたい。アメリカ国内のニュースだけではなく，「空からニュージーランドの氷河を見る」や「フランスで年金改革反対の抗議デモ」など，世界のニュースも含まれている。また，身近で親しみやすい話題としては，「用務員さんの引退をサポートする高校生」，考えさせる話題としては，「ChatGPTの開発者に聞く」などを収録した。

ニュースを収録した映像は、専用のウェブサイトplus+Media上でストリーミング視聴することができる。ぜひ，学生諸君にはこの映像を繰り返し見てもらいたい。アメリカの人々が家庭で毎日見ている良質のニュース番組に触れ，信頼できる情報をもとに英語を学んでもらいたい。

本書は1987年に *TV News from the U.S.A.* として始まった。その後，*ABC World News*, *Broadcast: ABC WORLD NEWS TONIGHT*，そして *ABC NEWSROOM* と

改良を重ねたロングシリーズとなっている。アメリカ ABC 放送のニュースを利用した本シリーズは，今回で通算31冊目になり，お陰様で長年にわたり毎回たいへん好評を頂いている。今後もより良い教材開発の努力を続けていきたい。

最後になったが，テキスト作成に際して毎回大変お世話になっている金星堂のみなさん，今回もこころよく版権を許可してくださったアメリカ ABC 放送に心から感謝の意を表したい。

2024年1月

山根　繁
Kathleen Yamane

Table of Contents •————————————————————————

News Story

1

Air Date: April 22, 2023
Duration: 1'41"

Honoring Earth Day

The Gist
■ What is Earth Day?
■ What did some young Americans do to celebrate it this year?

▶ **Before You Watch the News**   **Warm-up Exercises**

•)) **A Vocabulary Check:** Choose the correct definition for each of the words below.

🎧 DL 02   💿 CD1-02

1. eager   (   )   a. a tool for moving soil or snow
2. rehabilitate (   )   b. a particular group of living things
3. species   (   )   c. the most important factor
4. shovel   (   )   d. excited to do something
5. bottom line   (   )   e. restored to good health

B Fill in the blanks with appropriate expressions from the Vocabulary Check above. Change the word forms where necessary.

1. The monkey can't be released back into the wild until she has been completely
   (   ).
2. It might be easier to get rid of those small stones if you use a (   ).
3. We enjoyed watching several (   ) of rare birds at the zoo.
4. You're not going to the party unless you clean your room. And that's the
   (   )!
5. Jenny was (   ) to tell everyone about her trip to Puerto Rico.

W. Johnson: Finally tonight, on this Earth Day, the next generation eager to save the planet.

Earth Day was first celebrated on this day in 1970. People across the country gathered to raise awareness about environmental
5 issues. From the beginning, students have been front and center. That year, these teenagers leaving their cars at home to ride bikes instead. A third-grader shows a poster he made about air pollution. And today, the tradition continues. In the Florida Keys this morning, students learning [1.] _____
10 _____ , releasing
two rehabilitated sea turtles.

Teacher 1: ...on the top of that yellow flower...

W. Johnson: At this nursery in Tampa, Florida, young students taking a butterfly walk.

15 *Student 1:* We are learning about different types of species of butterflies and we're learning things that butterflies can do.

W. Johnson: Outside Chicago, preschoolers put on gloves, picked up shovels and got to work, planting petunias and dropping seeds in the soil,
[2.] _____
20 _____ .

Student 2: It is healthy and we can grow our bodies and get stronger.

Teacher 2: They can go home and ³· _____

_____ they want something green or something yellow or

red on their plates.

25 *W. Johnson:* Their experience continuing beyond the garden.

Student 3: I'm gonna clean up the trash today, ⁴· _____

_____.

Teacher 1: That's really the bottom line, is the more backyard national parks

we create, the better everything is.

30 *W. Johnson:* A new generation ⁵· _____

_____.

Student 4: Happy Earth Day!

Students, group: Happy Earth Day!

W. Johnson: Happy Earth Day. Good night.

Notes   L. 3   **Earth Day**   「アースデー；地球の日〈地球環境についての意識を高めるための日。毎年4月22日
に設定されている〉」

L. 5   **front and center**   「中心的存在」

L. 8   **Florida Keys**   「フロリダキーズ〈フロリダ州南岸沖に連なる一連の島々〉」

L. 13   **Tampa**   「タンパ〈フロリダ半島西中部に位置する都市〉」

L. 14   **butterfly walk**   「バタフライ・ウォーク；蝶の観察散歩〈タンパ市の南に位置する公園 Picnic
Island Park 内ではさまざまな種類の蝶の観察ができる〉」

L. 17   **preschoolers**   「未就学児［園児］たち〈保育園か幼稚園に通う子どもたち〉」

L. 18   **petunias**   「ペチュニア〈南米原産のナス科ペチュニア属に属する多年草〉」

L. 28   **That's really the bottom line, ... everything is.**   「＝That's really the bottom line. The
more backyard national parks we create, the better everything is.」

L. 28   **backyard national parks**   「裏庭の国立公園〈自宅の裏庭を，まるで国立公園のように自然豊か
にすることを言っている。自然や環境を大切にすることを小さい頃から自分の家の庭から始めれば，自
然に感謝する大人に育つだろうと考えている〉」

10

•)) **A** Listen to the news story and fill in the blanks in the text.

◉ CD1-03 [Normal]   ◉ CD1-04 [Slow]

B T/F Questions: Mark the following sentences true (T) or false (F) according to the information in the news story.

(   ) **1.** Earth Day has been celebrated for over 50 years.

(   ) **2.** Some teenagers made posters in honor of Earth Day.

(   ) **3.** Children in Florida rescued some sea turtles that needed rehabilitation.

(   ) **4.** The teacher is pleased that her students can identify the colors of the flowers they are growing.

(   ) **5.** Linking healthy eating with appreciating the planet is an important theme on Earth Day.

(   ) **6.** The young generation of Americans is eager to protect the earth.

•)) **C** Translate the following Japanese into English. Then listen to the CD and practice the conversation with your partner.   🎧 DL 03   ◉ CD1-05

A: Are you doing anything special for Earth Day this year?

B: Yeah. ¹. _____

_____ .

A: I don't mean the kids. I mean you!

B: Me? ². _____

_____ .

A: Oh, come on! We all need to take action to save our planet. Some of us are going to pick up trash along the river. Join us!

B: You're right. I will! ³. And _____

_____ .

A: Great. See you at 9:00.

1. 子どもたちは学校でポスターを作りましたし，明日彼らは自然観察ハイキングに行きます。

2. アースデーの意義は，地球を大切にする必要性をもっと子どもたちに知ってもらうことです。

3. それから，私はようやく裏庭に野菜を植えるつもりです。

•)) **D** **Summary Practice:** Fill in the blanks with suitable words beginning with the letters indicated. Then listen to the CD and check your answers.

DL 04   CD1-06

The first ($^{1.}$ **E**   ) ($^{2.}$ **D**   ) was celebrated on April 22, ($^{3.}$ **n**   )
($^{4.}$ **s**   ). Every year since, people have come together on that day to
($^{5.}$ **r**   ) ($^{6.}$ **a**   ) of the need to ($^{7.}$ **p**   ) the Earth.
All across the U.S., the ($^{8.}$ **y**   ) ($^{9.}$ **g**   ) is learning about
the ($^{10.}$ **e**   ) and ways to keep it healthy. Activities have
included making posters about ($^{11.}$ **a**   ) ($^{12.}$ **p**   ), learning about
($^{13.}$ **s**   ) ($^{14.}$ **t**   ) and ($^{15.}$ **s**   ) of butterflies and
($^{16.}$ **p**   ) flowers and vegetables. ($^{17.}$ **T**   ) got involved too,
riding ($^{18.}$ **b**   ) instead of driving. Everyone doing their part for Mother
Earth.

E **Discussion:** Share your ideas and opinions with your classmates.

1. Does Japan celebrate Earth Day? What kinds of activities take place on that day? Have you ever participated? Do an internet search to see what other countries take part in Earth Day.

2. The purpose of Earth Day is to raise awareness of environmental issues. What issues are Japanese people most concerned with? What are people in your community doing to help the environment?

News Story

2

Air Date: February 26, 2023
Duration: 2'15"

Student Loan Showdown

The Gist
- What kind of student loan program has President Biden proposed?
- Why are some people challenging his plan?

▶ **Before You Watch the News** | *Warm-up Exercises*

•)) **A Vocabulary Check:** Choose the correct definition for each of the words below.

🎧 DL 05   ◎ CD1-07

1. pivotal   (   )   a. permission
2. undermine   (   )   b. to weaken or threaten the effectiveness of something
3. eligible   (   )   c. entitled; having the right to do something
4. controversial (   )   d. causing disagreement; contentious
5. consent   (   )   e. very important; essential

B Fill in the blanks with appropriate expressions from the Vocabulary Check above. Change the word forms where necessary.

1. This app is not provided to anyone under 18 without parental (   ).
2. Why is the mayor's plan to repair the bridge so (   )? Everyone must realize how dangerous the bridge is.
3. With the election only months away, the summer campaign season will be (   ).
4. When Grandpa turned 70, he became (   ) for discounts on all public transportation.
5. Please don't disagree with me like that in front of the children. Actually, you're (   ) my attempts to teach them good manners.

W. Johnson: Back here in the U.S. and what could be a pivotal week for millions of Americans waiting for word on President Biden's student loan forgiveness plan. The Supreme Court will hear arguments in two key legal challenges that could undermine the administration's

5   efforts [1.] _____ . Here's ABC's Ike Ejiochi in Washington.

I. Ejiochi: The financial futures of up to 43 million eligible student loan borrowers are in a state of uncertainty tonight, as the Supreme Court prepares to hear two challenges to President Biden's

10   controversial campaign promise, federal student loan forgiveness.

Pedestrian 1: [2.] _____ , but it would certainly help a lot and relieve a lot of that burden.

Pedestrian 2: People knew what they were doing when they signed it and they should pay it off.

15   *I. Ejiochi:* About one in six adults in the U.S. holds federal student loan debt. $1.6 trillion and rising, the White House says. But their plan would grant up to $20,000 in federal debt relief to student borrowers who make less than $125,000 a year. The latest Quinnipiac poll shows 53 percent of Americans approve of the plan while 43 percent are

20   against it.

Like masters graduate Lissa Pettenati. [3.] _____

_____ wants the courts to permanently end Biden's plan.

She says she borrowed $80,000 and paid it off within seven years, and others should do the same.

Did anybody help you pay them off?

L. Pettenati, teacher: Nope, I paid them, I... because that's how I was raised. I mean, I was raised that you get an education and you get a job.

I. Ejiochi: The first challenge to Biden's plan is led by a group of Republican-led states that won their case in the lower courts. They call the program an illegal abuse of power, and a $430 billion giveaway without Congress' consent. The second challenge involves two borrowers who say they were unfairly [4.] _____ _____. But now, it's in the Supreme Court's hands.

Pedestrian 3: Especially if you're low income, first generation, sometimes a debt that you will have to take on can affect you and your family for years to come.

I. Ejiochi: The White House says of the 26 million people [5.] _____ _____, the government reviewed and authorized 16 million for relief, but no loan forgiveness was granted before the courts paused the program. The high court will begin hearing the challenges on Tuesday. Whit?

W. Johnson: A case with major implications. Ike, thank you.

Notes   L. 2   **student loan forgiveness plan**   「学生ローン返済免除措置計画」

L. 4   **legal challenges**   「訴訟；法的な異議申し立て」

L. 7   **financial futures**   「経済上の見通し；将来の生活」

L. 14   **pay it off**   「それ［学生ローン］を返済する」

L. 18   **Quinnipiac poll**   「クイニピアック大学の世論調査〈コネチカット州の同大学では，米国におけ
る政治問題などに関する世論調査を定期的に行っている〉」

L. 28   **Republican-led**   「共和党主導の」

L. 29   **lower courts**   「下級裁（判所）；下級審」

L. 30   **giveaway**   「ばらまき〈ここでは，学生ローンの返済義務免除［放棄］の政策が，莫大な金額を費
やして一部の人だけに利益をもたらす不公平な政策であるということを意味している〉」

L. 35   **first generation**   「第１世代〈家族の中で初めて大学に進学した［両親が大学の学位を持ってい
ない］学生のこと〉」

L. 36   **take on ~**   「（借金）を背負う」

Background of the News

　学生ローンの問題は，米国の大学授業料の高騰により，多くの学生がローンを借りなければ進学できない状況にあることが背景にある。大学授業料は年々増加傾向にあり，過去40年の間に約３倍に上がったといわれている。*U.S. News & World Report*によると，2022年度の公立４年生大学の平均授業料は（地元学生の場合）年間10,423ドル（約146万円），私立４年生大学は年間39,723ドル（約556万円）に及ぶ。授業料の高騰と所得格差の拡大により，多くの家庭にとって大学進学が難しくなっている。2023年１月24日付の『週刊エコノミスト』によると，学生ローン債務者の数は約4,300万人で，総額約１兆6,000億ドル（約224兆円）に及び，返済が困難な人々が多く存在しているという。

　2023年６月30日，米連邦最高裁 (the Supreme Court) は，バイデン政権が提案した学生ローン返済免除措置計画 (student loan forgiveness plan) を無効とする判断を示した（最高裁の保守派６人の判事が無効だと判断し，リベラル派３人はこれに反対した）。最高裁は，学生ローンの一部免除が連邦政府の権力乱用 (abuse of power) であり，明確な議会の承認を得ていないと指摘した。これにより，バイデン政権の肝いりの政策の実行が難しくなり，再選を目指すバイデン大統領にとって痛手となる可能性がある。

•)) **A** Listen to the news story and fill in the blanks in the text.

◉ CD1-08 [Normal] ◉ CD1-09 [Slow]

B **T/F Questions:** Mark the following sentences true (T) or false (F) according to the information in the news story.

(   ) **1.** The relief plan proposed by Biden would provide some financial relief for all student borrowers.

(   ) **2.** Biden's plan would cancel 100 percent of student loan debt for people with the lowest incomes.

(   ) **3.** If enacted, the student loan relief program would cost over $400 billion.

(   ) **4.** Some Republican-led states oppose the plan because students in their states were denied relief.

(   ) **5.** Following the review process, the government authorized 16 million applicants for debt relief.

(   ) **6.** The Supreme Court may decide to cancel the program even though over half of all Americans approve of it.

•)) **C** Translate the following Japanese into English. Then listen to the CD and practice the conversation with your partner. 🎧 DL 06   ◉ CD1-10

A: What do you think will happen with the student loan relief plan?

B: I was really counting on that money.[1.] _____

_____!

A: [2.] I know, but _____.

B: Yeah, but those people don't know what it's like for low-income people like me.

A: [3.] _____

_____.

B: Well, I guess anything that involves so much money is bound to be controversial.

A: A lot of people will be disappointed if the Supreme Court rules against it, that's for sure.

1. バイデン大統領は，そのプログラムを選挙公約に掲げていました。
2. 知っていますが，多くの人はそれが権力の乱用だと言っています。
3. 不当に救済を拒否されたと主張している借り手もいます。

•)) **D** **Summary Practice:** Fill in the blanks with suitable words beginning with the letters indicated. Then listen to the CD and check your answers.

DL 07   CD1-11

The U.S. (¹·**S**   ) (²·**C**   ) will soon begin hearing (³·**c**   )
to President Biden's (⁴·**f**   ) (⁵·**s**   ) (⁶·**l**   ) relief program.
While a slim majority of Americans support it, others say the (⁷·**f**   )
plan, which would give up to $ (⁸·**t**   ) (⁹·**t**   ) to some
borrowers, is an (¹⁰·**a**   ) of presidential (¹¹·**p**   ). Graduate Lissa
Pettenati is one of those who oppose the program. She repaid her loans herself, she
said, having been raised to believe that you get an (¹²·**e**   ) and then
you get a (¹³·**j**   ). With about (¹⁴·**o**   ) out of (¹⁵·**s**   ) adults in the U.S.
facing student loan (¹⁶·**d**   ), as many as 43 million (¹⁷·**e**   ) borrowers
could be affected if the program is (¹⁸·**u**   ). Millions of young
Americans are hoping the (¹⁹·**u**   ) is over soon.

E **Discussion:** Share your ideas and opinions with your classmates.

1. Compare the average cost of a four-year university education in the U.S. and in Japan. What kind of financial aid is available to students here? What percentage of students rely on student loans? Do they often have difficulty repaying those loans?

2. Some Americans approve of Biden's plan to lower the financial burden on student borrowers, but others, especially those who have already repaid their loans, are strongly against it. How do you feel about this issue? Discuss your opinions in a group.

3. The Supreme Court has the final say regarding many critical aspects of life in the U.S. Look for information on other issues that they have decided on during the past year.

"Biden" の発音

米大統領Biden /baɪdən/の発音は，アメリカ英語では/ə/が脱落して/ baɪdn/となることが多い。このように破裂音の/t/や/d/と鼻音の/n/が連続する場合は，呼気を鼻から開放する発音になるため「鼻腔開放」と呼ばれる。/d/の発音の際，舌先を上歯茎につけたまま，/n/を発音して「クッ」と鼻から呼気を抜くとこの発音ができる。この場合，Bidenは「バイデン」ではなく「バイ (ド) ゥン」のように聞こえる。

important /ɪmpɔːt(ə)nt/も，/ə/が脱落して/tn/の連鎖になることが多いため，「インポー(ト)ゥン」のように聞こえ，mountain /maunt(ə)n/も同様に「マウン(ト)ゥン」になる。

—…, as the Supreme Court prepares to hear two challenges to President *Biden's* controversial campaign promise, … *(Student Loan Showdown, P. 14 L. 8)*

—The first challenge to *Biden's* plan is led by a group of Republican-led states… *(Student Loan Showdown, P. 15 L. 28)*

—President *Biden* signing the landmark bipartisan Respect for Marriage Act, … *(Biden Signs Marriage Law, P. 38 L. 2)*

—Have they talked to the *Biden* administration about this? *(ChatGPT Technology, P. 66 L. 76)*

—Now to President *Biden's* move to approve a drilling project in Alaska, … *(Drilling Project in Alaska, P. 84 L. 1)*

—Why is it *important* to you that people know what's going on here? *(New Zealand Warning on Climate, P. 28 L. 38)*

—Stunning and really *important*. *(New Zealand Warning on Climate, P. 29 L. 45)*

—I think sports are very *important*… *(Sister Jean, the Beloved Chaplain, P. 73 L. 25)*

—Soaking in the majestic *mountains*. *(New Zealand Warning on Climate, P. 27 L. 12)*

—We wind our way around the Mexican *mountainside*, about 60 miles south of Mexico City, … *(Safe Drinking Water, P. 49 L. 10)*

Air Date: January 4, 2023
Duration: 1' 22"

Celebrating as American Citizens

The Gist
■ What is the Walker family celebrating?
■ What is special about their family?

▶ **Before You Watch the News** | *Warm-up Exercises*

•)) **A Vocabulary Check:** Choose the correct definition for each of the words below.

🎧 DL 08   ⊙ CD1-12

1. adopted ( ) **a.** nationality
2. citizenship ( ) **b.** loyalty; commitment
3. recite ( ) **c.** legally taken into a family and raised as one's own child
4. pledge ( ) **d.** an oath or promise
5. allegiance ( ) **e.** to repeat or say from memory in front of others

B Fill in the blanks with appropriate expressions from the Vocabulary Check above. Change the word forms where necessary.

1. Our Spanish teacher was so strict! She made us ( ) Spanish dialogues in class at the beginning of every lesson.
2. We all have to memorize the Girl Scout ( ) for tomorrow's ceremony.
3. Tomoko was born in France, so she has ( ) in two countries.
4. I was surprised to learn that Jerry was ( ). He looks just like his father!
5. All freshmen hoping to join the fraternity have to promise their ( ).

D. Muir: Finally tonight, two brothers, two birthday cakes and a wish come true.

Tonight, in Charlotte, North Carolina, the Walker family is celebrating. It has been an incredible journey [1.]_____

5   _____.

Family: Happy birthday to you!

D. Muir: In recent months, first, the birthday for Abraham. His reaction, pure joy. [2.] _____.
Abraham was adopted from Sierra Leone. A month later, ...

10 *Family:* Happy birthday, dear James!

D. Muir: ...Abraham's big brother James, it was his turn. The Walkers are now a family of eight. First came the birthdays, then the U.S. citizenship ceremony, signing the paperwork, [3.] _____
_____, and reciting the Pledge of

15   Allegiance. Then Christmas and the new year together. And right here, tonight...

Family: Hi, David.

D. Muir: ...James and his new mother Jamie on being a U.S. citizen.

J. Walker: It makes me feel like I'm already born in this country, and [4.]_____

20   _____, here.

Mother: Yes, you do.

D. Muir: James tells us his brother is already practicing with the new team at school, and the Walkers on their hope for this new year ahead.

J. Walker: I'm pretty excited to, like, ^{5.} _____

25   _____ .

Family: Yeah!

D. Muir: A family forever. Good night.

Notes   L. 3   **Charlotte** 「シャーロット〈米国ノースカロライナ州最大の都市〉」

          L. 9   **Sierra Leone** 「シエラ・レオネ〈大西洋に面した西アフリカの国で，北東はギニア，南東はリベリアと国境を接している〉」

          L. 23   **on their hope for ~** 「～への希望を語った」

•)) **A** Listen to the news story and fill in the blanks in the text.

         ⊙ CD1-13 [Normal]   ⊙ CD1-14 [Slow]

B **T/F Questions:** Mark the following sentences true (T) or false (F) according to the information in the news story.

(   ) **1.** All of the Walker children were adopted from Sierra Leone.

(   ) **2.** The citizenship ceremony took place in Sierra Leone.

(   ) **3.** Both of the Walkers' adopted children now have U.S. citizenship.

(   ) **4.** Abraham and James are now officially members of the Walker family.

(   ) **5.** James Walker is now practicing with a new team at his school.

(   ) **6.** James wants to relax for a while after his busy year.

•)) **C** Translate the following Japanese into English. Then listen to the CD and practice the conversation with your partner.   🎧 DL 09   ⊙ CD1-15

A: How was the birthday party, Jamie?

B: Wonderful! ¹· _____

_____ .

A: It was probably the first one he ever had.

B: It was. And soon it will be James' birthday.

A: ²· _____ .

B: Really! ³· And _____

_____ .

A: You should be really proud of them both. And of yourselves, for creating such a great family!

1. エイブラハムは自分のバースデーケーキを見て嬉し涙を流しました。

2. 今年はあなたの家族にとって初めてのことがとても多くありましたね。

3. そして，あの素晴らしい息子たちは，これからもすべてのことをより良くしていこうと決意しています。

•)) **D** **Summary Practice:** Fill in the blanks with suitable words beginning with the letters indicated. Then listen to the CD and check your answers.

DL 10   CD1-16

Jamie Walker and her husband from Charlotte, North Carolina are now the proud parents of ($^{1.}$**s**   ) children. Originally from ($^{2.}$**S**   ) ($^{3.}$**L**   ), their ($^{4.}$**a**   ) sons James and Abraham had their U.S. ($^{5.}$**c**   ) ($^{6.}$**c**   ) last year, completing the necessary ($^{7.}$**p**   ) and reciting the ($^{8.}$**P**   ) of ($^{9.}$**A**   ). There were also ($^{10.}$**b**   ) to celebrate, as well as ($^{11.}$**C**   ) and the arrival of the ($^{12.}$**n**   ) ($^{13.}$**y**   ). It was a long ($^{14.}$**j**   ) but for this amazing family of ($^{15.}$**e**   ), their ($^{16.}$**w**   ) has finally come true.

E **Discussion:** Share your ideas and opinions with your classmates.

1. The news story does not explain why Abraham and James were adopted from Sierra Leone. Can you imagine what the circumstances might be? Talk with a partner and share your ideas.

2. Do an internet search to find out what is required to become a U.S. citizen. What are the requirements for Japanese citizenship?

3. Is adoption common in Japan? Look for statistics on the number of adoptions annually in Japan, the U.S. and one other country.

箇条書き的な表現

　ニュースの英語では，一般動詞，be動詞，関係代名詞などを省略し，箇条書き的な表現で情報を生き生きと伝えることが多い。文法より伝達する意味内容を重視するため，短い語句をたたみかけるように次々にことばをつなぐのである。特に，ニュースの冒頭の部分で，何についての報道であるか，そのトピックを告げるときにこの手法はよく用いられる。新聞英語の「見出し」のような役割を果たしているといえる。

　例えば，以下の例では外国から養子に迎えられた二人の兄弟が，それぞれの誕生日の後，アメリカ市民権を取得したニュースを伝えている。ニュースの冒頭では，見出しとしてニュースのキーワードである"birthday cakes"と"wish"を用いて端的に伝えられている。他の例でもニュースのキーワードが示されているため，冒頭に注目するとニュースを理解するうえで助けになる。

—Finally tonight, two brothers, two birthday cakes and a wish come true.

(Celebrating as American Citizens, P.21 L.1)

—We turn now to the White House, and the historic moment today.

(Biden Signs Marriage Law, P.38 L.1)

—Finally tonight here, the teacher, her dog, and the students who were determined to do something. *(Students Create Prosthesis for Dog, P.57 L.1)*

—Finally, tonight, "America Strong." Sister Jean, the beloved chaplain, sharing her incredible story. *(Sister Jean, the Beloved Chaplain, P.72 L.1)*

New Zealand Warning on Climate

The Gist
- Why did ABC's Robin Roberts visit New Zealand?
- What did she witness there?

▶ **Before You Watch the News**   *Warm-up Exercises*

•)) **A Vocabulary Check:** Choose the correct definition for each of the words below.

🎧 DL 11   ⊙ CD1-17

1. vanish   (   )   a. a narrow opening
2. suit up   (   )   b. incredibly large and beautiful
3. soak in   (   )   c. to put on a uniform; to dress to prepare to do something
4. majestic   (   )   d. to disappear
5. crevice   (   )   e. to enjoy the atmosphere of a special place

B Fill in the blanks with appropriate expressions from the Vocabulary Check above. Change the word forms where necessary.

1. Where are my glasses? They always (   ) when I need them.
2. If you want to walk under the waterfall with us, you'll have to (   ). There's an extra set of rain gear in the car.
3. Squirrels hide their acorns in the (   ) of that big maple tree.
4. I enjoy traveling with Missy, but sometimes she talks too much when I just want to (   ) the scenery.
5. The highlight of our trip was seeing the (   ) redwood trees.

▶ Focus on the News Story

D. Muir: Finally, tonight here, ABC News and our reporting on climate. Robin
Roberts taking us to New Zealand for the wonder of it all and the
warning about what's changing already.

R. Roberts: To get an up-close look at New Zealand's spectacular yet
5 vanishing glaciers...

So, this is the bird we're going up in.

M. Clarke, glacier pilot: Certainly is.

R. Roberts: We suited up for a bird's-eye view, ¹·_____
_____ the dangerously thin ice, an out-of-this-world
10 experience.

Here we go.

Soaking in the majestic mountains.

So untouched. Just so natural.

Crystal blue lakes.

15 Oh, my goodness.

And breathtaking waterfalls.

Wow.

Our larger-than-life trek revealing ²·_____
_____ . Glacier pilot Michael Clarke.

20 *M. Clarke:* It looks like a waterfall, but that's actually ice all falling off the cliffs and smashing. So, you can see them just disappearing right in front of our eyes.

R. Roberts: Behind the stunning landscape lie cracks and crevices. **3.** _____
_____.

25 *M. Clarke:* I can tell you I've watched glaciers completely disappear throughout my career.

R. Roberts: Over 6,000 feet above sea level, it was time to experience the glacier's conditions first-hand.

Wow.

30 *M. Clarke:* Welcome to paradise.

R. Roberts: Thank you, Michael. Are you kidding me? Nice office you got here.

M. Clarke: It's a pretty good office.

R. Roberts: Oh, my gosh. **4.** _____.

M. Clarke: You are. And it's quite soft, even for this time of the morning. Look
35 at that.

R. Roberts: Yes.

M. Clarke: Just a little bit after 9:00 a.m. and it's warm.

R. Roberts: Why is it important to you that people know what's going on here?

40　*M. Clarke:* Well, **5.** _____
.

I bring tourists from all around the world to appreciate and look at these beautiful glaciers. But once they're gone, obviously, we won't be able to do that anymore.

R. Roberts: Bright sun, soft ice, and extraordinary views on top of the ice.

45　*D. Muir:* Stunning and really important. Robin from New Zealand again tomorrow first thing on *GMA*. I'll see you tomorrow night. Good night.

Notes　L. 6　**the bird**　「ヘリコプター〈鳥瞰図をとるための乗りもの〉」

L. 8　**bird's-eye view**　「鳥瞰図；上空から見渡す景色」

L. 9　**out-of-this-world**　「この世のものとは思えないくらい（素晴らしい）」

L. 13　**untouched**　「手付かずの」

L. 18　**larger-than-life**　「非常に印象的な；壮大な」

L. 28　**first-hand**　「直接に」

L. 31　**Are you kidding me?**　「冗談ですよね？〈氷河の上で目にした光景に感動している〉」

L. 31　**Nice office you got here.**　「良いオフィスですね〈ヘリコプターのパイロットであるクラークさんは氷河を「仕事場」としているので，氷河をオフィスと呼んでいる〉」

L. 46　*GMA*　「= Good Morning America〈ABC で放送されている朝の情報番組〉」

▶　**After You Watch the News**　　*Exercises*

•)) **A** Listen to the news story and fill in the blanks in the text.

◎ CD1-18 [Normal]　◎ CD1-19 [Slow]

B **T/F Questions:** Mark the following sentences true (T) or false (F) according to the information in the news story.

(　　) **1.** What appear from above to be waterfalls are sometimes melting ice.

(　　) **2.** The ice is thin because the glaciers are melting.

(　　) **3.** Michael Clarke has not yet seen a glacier disappear, but he warns that that could happen soon.

(　　) **4.** Robin Roberts walked on a glacier 6,000 feet above sea level.

(　　) **5.** According to Michael Clarke, the glaciers tend to be softer and warmer early in the day.

(　　) **6.** Robin Roberts hopes to start bringing tourists to New Zealand to learn about climate change.

•)) **C** Translate the following Japanese into English. Then listen to the CD and practice the conversation with your partner. 🎧 DL 12 💿 CD1-20

A: Robin, how was your trip to New Zealand?

B: Great! [1.] _____.

A: And did you actually get to see the glaciers?

B: I was standing on them! But there's a downside to the story as well.

A: What do you mean?

B: [2.] _____. They could vanish!

A: [3.] _____

_____. It's time to get serious about it!

1. 景色が本当に素晴らしかったです。

2. それらの壮観な氷河が溶けているのです。

3. 気候変動は，私たちの雄大な世界の多くを破壊しています。

•)) **D** **Summary Practice:** Fill in the blanks with suitable words beginning with the letters indicated. Then listen to the CD and check your answers.

🎧 DL 13 💿 CD1-21

ABC's Robin Roberts joined ([1.] **g** _____) ([2.] **p** _____) Michael Clarke in ([3.] **N** ____) ([4.] **Z** _____) to learn more about climate change. ([5.] **S** _____) ([6.] **u** ____) for the helicopter ride, Roberts enjoyed a ([7.] **b** _____)-([8.] **e** _____) ([9.] **v** _____) of the ([10.] **m** _____) mountains and ([11.] **c** _____) ([12.] **b** ____) lakes below. The pilot explained that what appeared to be breathtaking ([13.] **w** _____) were in fact chunks of ([14.] **i** ____) falling from the cliffs—ice which is currently melting at a ([15.] **r** _____) ([16.] **r** _____). For now, Robin Roberts and Clarke's other ([17.] **t** _____) can ([18.] **s** _____) ([19.] **i** ____) the spectacular beauty of the glaciers, but if climate change continues, they could ([20.] **v** _____) before too long.

E **Discussion:** Share your ideas and opinions with your classmates.

1. This news story is part of ABC's special series on climate. Have you seen other news shows or documentaries aiming to make the public more aware of climate change? What other efforts are being made to educate people about the growing threats?

2. How much do you know about glaciers? How are they formed? Where can they be found? Are there any glaciers in Asia? Check on the internet and see what you can learn. Share your findings with the class.

Students Help 80-Year-Old Janitor

The Gist
- What was the janitor's problem?
- How were the students able to help him?

▶ **Before You Watch the News** | *Warm-up Exercises*

•)) **A Vocabulary Check:** Choose the correct definition for each of the words below.

🎧 DL 14   ⊙ CD1-22

1. retiree   (   )   a. at the beginning; first
2. caption   (   )   b. a short written explanation attached to a photo or video
3. cushion   (   )   c. to show or exhibit
4. initial   (   )   d. a person who no longer works, usually due to advanced
5. display   (   )   age
                           e. something that softens the impact

B Fill in the blanks with appropriate expressions from the Vocabulary Check above. Change the word forms where necessary.

1. His (   ) reaction was negative, but I think Jerry is coming around to the idea of spending the whole summer at the lake.
2. We should have a financial (   ) in case there's another pandemic.
3. Katy has always (   ) a talent for imitating animal sounds.
4. Our neighborhood association started a new social club for (   ).
5. It's important to pay attention to the (   ) under the photos in the book.

D. Muir: Finally, tonight, he was retired. But like so many retirees, bills going up. So, at 80, he showed up at school to work as the janitor. The students noticed.

Tonight, in Callisburg, Texas, north of Dallas-Fort Worth, the students at Callisburg High School have done something extraordinary for their beloved janitor, Mr. James. Mr. James Gailey is 80 years old. And like so many retirees, he came out of retirement 1. _____. Principal Jason Hooper.

J. Hooper, principal, Callisburg High School: He shared with me that his rent within a year has gone up nearly $400 and he just couldn't afford to continue paying without going back to work.

D. Muir: Senior, Greyson Thurman.

G. Thurman, senior, Callisburg High School: 2. _____

_____, it broke my heart because nobody at 80 should be working. They should be living the rest of their life.

D. Muir: So, the students had an idea. Taking this video of Mr. James and posting it online with the caption, "This is our 80-year-old janitor who had his rent raised and had to come back to work. Let's help Mr. James out." Senior Marti Yousko.

M. Yousko, senior, Callisburg High School: We're just hoping that 3. _____

_____, you know, might give him a little bit of cushion, a little bit more comfort.

D. Muir: Tonight, now two-and-a-half weeks after their initial post, the incredible response. So many people moved by what the students
25 did, they began donating to Mr. James on GoFundMe. More than 8,000 donations from all over the country now, more than $270,000. And ^{4.}_____,
Mr. James is going back into retirement. And right here tonight, the principal.

30 *J. Hooper:* Hey, David.

D. Muir: Principal Hooper on his students, who recognized need and acted.

J. Hooper: We're so thankful that we have kids who look out for others, ^{5.}_____, and who display kindness in every way that they possibly can.

35 *D. Muir:* We're counting on this next generation. They sure stepped up. Good night.

Notes   L. 1 **bills** 「(家賃などの) 請求額；生活費」
        L. 4 **Callisburg** 「カリスバーグ〈テキサス州の北部に位置する都市〉」
        L. 4 **Dallas-Fort Worth** 「ダラス・フォートワース (複合都市圏)〈フォートワースはダラスの西に位置する。両市はテキサス州北部にあり，複合都市圏を構成している〉」
        L. 7 **came out of ~** 「~から復帰する」
        L. 9 **shared with me** 「私に話してくれた」
        L. 25 **GoFundMe** 「ゴーファンドミー〈2010年創業の寄付型クラウドファンディング〉」
        L. 31 **on his students** 「彼の生徒について語ってくれた」
        L. 32 **look out for ~** 「~に気を配る；~を気にかける」
        L. 35 **stepped up** 「(人助けをして) ステップアップした；活躍した」

•)) **A** Listen to the news story and fill in the blanks in the text.

⊚ CD1-23 [Normal] ⊚ CD1-24 [Slow]

B **T/F Questions:** Mark the following sentences true (T) or false (F) according to the information in the news story.

(   ) **1.** Principal Hooper asked the students to collect money for Mr. James.

(   ) **2.** Mr. James returned to work because he loved his job and the students at Callisburg High School.

(   ) **3.** The janitor's rent went up dramatically in less than a year.

(   ) **4.** The students used social media to collect donations for their janitor.

(   ) **5.** It took several months, but the students received donations totaling $270,000 from GoFundMe.

(   ) **6.** The principal was not happy that the students posted personal information about the school janitor online.

•)) **C** Translate the following Japanese into English. Then listen to the CD and practice the conversation with your partner.   🎧 DL 15   ⊚ CD1-25

A: Have you seen our GoFundMe site?

B: I haven't checked it yet. We just put it up a couple weeks ago.

A: ¹· _____

_____ !

B: You're joking!

A: No! ²· _____ .

B: ³· _____

_____ .

A: And by what *we* did! I'm so glad we can help him!

1. 全国から8,000件以上の寄付が集まってきています！

2. こんなに反響があるとは全く思っていませんでした。

3. ジェームスさんの話に感動した人が多かったのでしょうね。

•)) **D** **Summary Practice:** Fill in the blanks with suitable words beginning with the letters indicated. Then listen to the CD and check your answers.

Jason Hooper, the ($^{1.}$ **p**   ) of Callisburg ($^{2.}$ **H**   ) ($^{3.}$ **S**   ) in ($^{4.}$ **T**   ), is feeling mighty proud of his ($^{5.}$ **s**   ) tonight. The school's beloved ($^{6.}$ **j**   ), ($^{7.}$ **e**   )-year-old James Gailey, was a ($^{8.}$ **r**   ) who had to return to ($^{9.}$ **w**   ) because his ($^{10.}$ **r**   ) was raised by nearly $400 and he was unable to pay his ($^{11.}$ **b**   ). Senior Greyson Thurman says it ($^{12.}$ **b**   ) his ($^{13.}$ **h**   ) to see Mr. James still working, when he should be ($^{14.}$ **l**   ) the rest of his life. The students had the idea of posting a ($^{15.}$ **v**   ) of Mr. James ($^{16.}$ **o**   ) and starting a GoFundMe site, quickly raising $270,000 with ($^{17.}$ **d**   ) from all over America. Mr. Hooper is thankful to have students who ($^{18.}$ **d**   ) such kindness.

E **Discussion:** Share your ideas and opinions with your classmates.

1. Do you know any people in their 80s who work? What kinds of jobs do elderly people in Japan do? Do you think it's good for retirees to continue working? Discuss the pros and cons with your classmates.

2. Look for other news stories about students who find creative ways to help others. Have you or anyone around you ever been involved in such a project?

News Story
6

Air Date: December 13, 2022
Duration: 2' 05"

Biden Signs Marriage Law

The Gist
- Who will be affected by the marriage law signed by the president?
- What will the new law do for those people? What won't it do?

▶ **Before You Watch the News**   *Warm-up Exercises*

•)) **A** **Vocabulary Check:** Choose the correct definition for each of the words below.

🎧 DL 17   ◎ CD1-27

1. landmark	(	)	a.	to agree; to share the same opinion
2. interracial	(	)	b.	essential; necessary
3. vital	(	)	c.	an assertion or idea
4. proposition	(	)	d.	an event marking a major turning point
5. concur	(	)	e.	involving two or more different races

B Fill in the blanks with appropriate expressions from the Vocabulary Check above. Change the word forms where necessary.

1. If enough members (   ) with Ken's plan, we should be able to finish up the project this month.

2. (   ) conflict is of great concern in many parts of the world.

3. It is (   ) that the results of the polling remain secret until the official announcement is made.

4. In a (   ) case, the judge ruled in favor of the drug company.

5. The mayor's (   ) is quite reasonable. In the long run, we'd save thousands of dollars by repairing the bridges now rather than waiting.

D. Muir: We turn now to the White House, and the historic moment today. President Biden signing the landmark bipartisan Respect for Marriage Act, protecting same-sex and interracial marriages in this country, saying, quote, "This law and the love it defends strike a

5   blow against hate in all its forms." This had bipartisan support. Twelve Republicans in the Senate, 39 Republicans in the House joining the Democrats [1.] _____

_____. Mary Bruce at the White House.

M. Bruce: Today, in front of a joyous crowd of thousands, President Biden

10   signing into law protections for same-sex and interracial marriage.

President J. Biden: Today's a good day. A day America takes a vital step toward equality.

M. Bruce: Biden today noting [2.] _____ since he publicly supported same-sex marriage ahead of his boss, then-

15   President Obama.

President J. Biden: Marriage is a simple proposition. Who do you love, and will you be loyal with that person you love? [3.] _____

_____. The law recognized that everyone should have the right to answer those questions for

20   themselves without the government interference.

M. Bruce: The Respect for Marriage Act is an effort to protect marriage after the Supreme Court overturned Roe v. Wade in June. In his concurring opinion, Justice Clarence Thomas called on the court to

reconsider decisions that legalized same-sex marriage. The new law
does not guarantee the right to marry, but it does require states to
honor and recognize all marriages.

President J. Biden: It's one thing for the Supreme Court to rule on a case. But
it's another thing entirely for elected representatives of the people
to take a vote on the floor of the United States Congress and ^{4.}____
_____ , "Love is love. Right is right.
Justice is justice."

M. Bruce: Now, polls do show that more than 70 percent of Americans support
same-sex marriage, and this was a bipartisan victory, though the
majority of Republicans opposed it, arguing ^{5.}_____
_____ . David?

D. Muir: Mary Bruce, who was on the air with us for this late this afternoon.
Mary, thank you.

Notes L. 2 **bipartisan** 「超党派の」
L. 2 **Respect for Marriage Act** 「結婚尊重法案〈同性婚のほか、これまで連邦法で合法化されていなかった異なる人種同士の結婚の権利も擁護されることが明記された〉」
L. 4 **strike a blow against ~** 「~に打撃を与える；~に対抗する」
L. 6 **the Senate** 「(米国議会の) 上院」
L. 6 **the House** 「(米国議会の) 下院」
L. 14 **his boss** 「上司〈バイデン大統領は8年間にわたり副大統領として当時のオバマ大統領を支えた〉」
L. 22 **Roe v. Wade** 「ロー対ウェイド判決〈最高裁は1973年1月、人工妊娠中絶を憲法で保障された権利として初めて認めた。その結果、中絶はアメリカ合衆国の全50州で合法化されていた。ロー対ウェイドという判決の名は、この重要な裁判に関わった2人の主要な当事者の名前に由来している〉」
L. 23 **Justice Clarence Thomas** 「クラレンス・トーマス最高裁判事〈同判事は、ロー対ウェイド判決にも反対して中絶の権利を否定していた〉」
L. 23 **called on ~** 「~に求めた [要求した]」
L. 27 **rule on ~** 「~に判決を下す」
L. 36 **on the air** 「番組に出演する」

Background of the News

　2022年12月13日，同性婚の権利保護法案である結婚尊重法案（Respect for Marriage Act）が可決され，バイデン大統領が署名して成立した。米国では各州が婚姻に関する権限を有しており，2004年にマサチューセッツ州で初めて同性婚が合法化されて以降多くの州で認められるようになったが，連邦レベルでの合法化には至っていなかった。

　この法案は同性婚慎重派の多い共和党議員からの賛成票も一部あり、成立に至った。法案提出の背景には，2022年6月に連邦最高裁がロー対ウェイド判決を覆したことが挙げられる。この判決後，最高裁が次は同性婚に対しても同様の動きに出ることを懸念し，バイデン政権は法整備を急いだ。同法は，合法の州で成立した婚姻が全州で保護されるという内容も盛り込まれており，今後の最高裁による影響を最小限に抑えられるように先手を打った。バイデン大統領はこの法案の成立を歓迎し，さらなる平等と自由の実現への一歩と位置づけた。

　同性婚の権利保護の動きは世界的にも広がっており，近年ではキューバや一部のアジア諸国などでも同性婚が合法化されている。一方，日本では2023年6月16日，LGBTなど性的少数者らへの理解増進法が参院本会議で成立したものの，同性婚に関する法整備は進んでいない。今後，同性婚や性的少数者の権利保護に向けた法的な取り組みの一層の進展が求められている。

▶ **After You Watch the News**　　*Exercises*

•)) **A** Listen to the news story and fill in the blanks in the text.

◉ CD1-28 [Normal]　◉ CD1-29 [Slow]

B **T/F Questions:** Mark the following sentences true (T) or false (F) according to the information in the news story.

(　　) **1.** The new marriage law had the support of equal numbers of Republican representatives in the House and Senate.

(　　) **2.** President Biden claimed that the new law is an important step towards equality in the U.S.

(　　) **3.** Biden did not support same-sex marriage when he was vice-president, but now he does.

(   ) **4.** Justice Thomas would like the Supreme Court to reconsider the legality of same-sex marriage.

(   ) **5.** The Respect for Marriage Act guarantees that same-sex and interracial marriage will be allowed in every state in the U.S.

(   ) **6.** Seven out of 10 Americans believe that same-sex marriage should be legalized.

•)) **C** Translate the following Japanese into English. Then listen to the CD and practice the conversation with your partner. 🎧 DL 18 💿 CD1-30

A: Look at that crowd! You can feel the joy.

B: I just don't get it. What's the big deal?

A: Are you kidding? ¹· _____ .

B: Why do we need a law about who you can marry?

A: ²· With the new law, _____

_____ .

B: ³· Yeah, but _____

_____ .

A: You're so naïve!

1. 結婚尊重法案は画期的な法律です。

2. この新しい法律によって，全50州がすべての結婚を尊重し，認めることが求められるようになりました。

3. そうだけど，アメリカ人の大多数はすでに同性婚を支持しています。

•)) **D** **Summary Practice:** Fill in the blanks with suitable words beginning with the letters indicated. Then listen to the CD and check your answers.

🎧 DL 19 💿 CD1-31

A huge crowd was at the (¹· **W**   ) (²· **H**   ) today as President Biden signed the (³· **l**   ) Respect for (⁴· **M**   ) (⁵· **A**   ). The big theme of the day was (⁶· **l**   ), with Biden stressing that marriage should simply be about being (⁷· **l**   ) to the person you love. Passed with (⁸· **b**   ) (⁹· **s**   ) in both the (¹⁰· **S**   ) and the House, the new law falls short of guaranteeing that (¹¹· **s**   )-(¹²· **s**   ) and (¹³· **i**   ) couples can legally marry throughout the U.S., but it does (¹⁴· **r**   ) that all marriages be recognized—and that's a (¹⁵· **v**   ) step towards equality.

E **Discussion:** Share your ideas and opinions with your classmates.

1. How do you feel about the Respect for Marriage Act? What is the current situation of the LGBTQ community in Japan? Has it changed at all in recent years? Discuss your answers in a group.

2. Joseph Biden has long supported same-sex marriage. Look for information on other issues that he supports and laws that have been passed during his presidency.

News Story

7

Air Date: December 23, 2022
Duration: 1' 42"

David's Toy Project

The Gist
- How did David's Toy Project start?
- How successful has it been?

▶ **Before You Watch the News** **Warm-up Exercises**

•)) **A Vocabulary Check:** Choose the correct definition for each of the words below.

🎧 DL 20   💿 CD1-32

1. survivor	(	)	a.	brother or sister
2. a bunch of	(	)	b.	money or goods given to a charity
3. donation	(	)	c.	a large number of the same kind of things
4. extended	(	)	d.	expanded; longer
5. sibling	(	)	e.	a person who remains alive after a serious illness or accident

B Fill in the blanks with appropriate expressions from the Vocabulary Check above. Change the word forms where necessary.

1. After the Smiths lost their house in a fire, the neighbors collected (   ).
2. Meg found (   ) valuable old comic books in the attic.
3. Their grandfather taught Danny and his (   ) how to play chess.
4. Unfortunately, the police report on the explosion indicated that there were no (   ).
5. We usually only go away for three or four days, but let's take an (   ) vacation next year for our tenth wedding anniversary.

W. Johnson: Finally, tonight, "America Strong." The young cancer survivor who's already spent half his life delivering holiday cheer.

Twelve-year-old David Lauritzen is on a mission. The young cancer survivor from Katy, Texas picking out toys for children with cancer who will be in the hospital on Christmas. He calls it David's Toy Project. He got the idea six years ago, and [1.] _____ _____, he went to work.

Mother: He always made sure that everybody had a toy in the cancer center.

W. Johnson: It all started with a simple jar to collect coins.

A. Lauritzen, David's Toy Project: In 2016, [2.] _____ _____, he collected $1,100. By 2018, it was $11,000. And I'm happy to say, as of right now, we're $3,000 short of $100,000.

W. Johnson: A hundred thousand dollars, and tens of thousands of toys over the years.

D. Lauritzen, David's Toy Project: [3.] _____, we just do, like, a bunch of collection stands. We just say, basically, ask around, people that are passing by, like hope that we get some donation.

W. Johnson: The project now so successful, it involves his extended family and friends.

SAMANTHA LAURITZEN
David's Toy Project

A. Lauritzen: It shifted from David's collecting toys to David and his siblings
and friends are all now **4.** _____

_____ .

Mother: I am beyond proud to have a child that can go through something

25　　　　like he did, go through cancer, and to be able to go through all of
　　　　that and still want to make a difference.

W. Johnson: And tonight, David's holiday message for all of us.

D. Lauritzen: I encourage everyone to do their part to make a positive
　　　　difference around you. Merry Christmas to all, and don't forget to

30　　　　give back, all year long.

W. Johnson: And that's what **5.** _____

_____ . I'm Whit Johnson in New York. Have a great night, and
happy holidays.

Notes　L. 1　**America Strong**　「アメリカ・ストロング〈「強くあれ，アメリカ」という心温まるニュース，ア
　　　　　　メリカを元気にしてくれるニュースを紹介するコーナー〉」

　　　L. 4　**Katy**　「ケイティ〈テキサス州の東南部に位置するヒューストンの西隣の街〉」

　　　L. 4　**picking out ~**　「~を選んでいる」

　　　L. 5　**David's Toy Project**　「デイビッドのおもちゃプロジェクト」

　　　L. 12　**~ short of ...**　「…にあと~足りない」

　　　L. 16　**like ~**　「その~；まあ；~という感じで；例えば；何か〈つなぎ言葉として，くだけた会話の中で
　　　　　　よく使われる〉」

　　　L. 16　**collection stands**　「募金箱」

　　　L. 16　**We just say, basically, ask around, ... get some donation.**　「= Basically we just talk to
　　　　　　people passing by and hope we can get donations. と言いたかったと思われる。〈これは，子ども
　　　　　　の発話のため文法的ではない。また，デイビッド君の "ask" の発音は k と s が反転しているため「ア
　　　　　　クス」に聞こえるが，子どもにありがちな発音になっている〉」

　　　L. 24　**beyond proud**　「この上なく（ただただ）誇りに思う」

　　　L. 24　**go through ~**　「（困難やつらいことなどを）経験する」

•)) **A** Listen to the news story and fill in the blanks in the text.

◎ CD1-33 [Normal]   ◎ CD1-34 [Slow]

B **Multiple Choice Questions:** Select the best answer to each question.

1. David Lauritzen has spent half his life

   a. in the hospital undergoing cancer treatments.

   b. collecting donations for hospitalized children.

   c. collecting money to donate for cancer research.

2. The Toy Project started

   a. with a jar of coins.

   b. while David was undergoing cancer treatment.

   c. both *a* and *b*.

3. Today, David's Toy Project relies on

   a. donations from his extended family.

   b. big donations during the Christmas season.

   c. collection stands and a team of helpers.

4. David's mother is proud that her son

   a. has found clever ways to collect such a large amount of money.

   b. is on a mission to help other children become cancer survivors.

   c. cares so much for others when he has been through such a difficult time himself.

•)) **C** Translate the following Japanese into English. Then listen to the CD and practice the conversation with your partner.   🎧 DL 21   ◎ CD1-35

A: Look! There's the collection stand. Let's go donate.

B: Donate for what?

A: It's David's Toy Project. 1._____

_____.

B: Wow! How can one boy do all that?

A: He's not working alone. ^{2.} _____

_____.

B: That's amazing. ^{3.} _____.

A: Come on! We can make a difference, too.

1. 彼はがんを克服した人で，がんセンターの子どもたちにクリスマスのおもちゃを買うために寄付を集めています。

2. このプロジェクトはとても大きくなって，今では彼の親戚や友達も参加しています。

3. 彼らは本当に良い変化をもたらしています。

•)) **D** **Summary Practice:** Fill in the blanks with suitable words beginning with the letters indicated. Then listen to the CD and check your answers.

🎧 DL 22   💿 CD1-36

"America Strong" focuses on a special 12-year old from (¹·**T**_____) who is on a (²·**m**_____) to cheer up (³·**c**_____) who are hospitalized at (⁴·**C**_____). A (⁵·**c**_____) (⁶·**s**_____) himself, David Lauritzen set out to make sure that every child in the cancer center had a (⁷·**t**____) for the holidays. When his own (⁸·**t**_____) finished, David started his project by collecting (⁹·**c**_____) in a simple (¹⁰·**j**____). Since 2016, David's Toy Project has grown so big that he now needs the assistance of his (¹¹·**e**_____) family and friends to work the collection (¹²·**s**_____) throughout the year and select toys for the sick children. This year they have collected nearly $(¹³·**o**____) (¹⁴·**h**_____) (¹⁵·**t**_____). David's mother is rightfully (¹⁶·**p**_____) of her son for wanting to make a difference—and so are we!

E **Discussion:** Share your ideas and opinions with your classmates.

1. This news story was aired just before Christmas in 2022. Do an internet search to learn more about David Lauritzen and see if his Toy Project is still going strong.

2. Look for other stories about people who have found ways to help others in need.

Safe Drinking Water

The Gist	■ What are some solutions to obtaining safe drinking water?
	■ How big a problem is accessing drinking water worldwide?

▶ **Before You Watch the News**   *Warm-up Exercises*

•)) **A** **Vocabulary Check:** Choose the correct definition for each of the words below.

🎧 DL 23   ◉ CD2-02

1. dire   (   )   a. to change; to transform
2. viable   (   )   b. to think of; to imagine
3. pipe dream   (   )   c. disastrous; awful
4. conceive of   (   )   d. feasible; possible
5. convert   (   )   e. something that seems very difficult to achieve

B Fill in the blanks with appropriate expressions from the Vocabulary Check above. Change the word forms where necessary.

1. Before your flight, be sure to (   ) some yen into the local currency.
2. The recent advances in AI technology were impossible to (   ) even five years ago.
3. If you don't get credit for your math class, there will be (   ) consequences.
4. Becoming a lawyer was really just a (   ) for Ken, but now he's opening his own law office.
5. The committee likes your idea, but we don't think it would be (   ) in such a hot climate.

L. Davis: We turn now to the water crisis on our planet. It's becoming more dire, and the search for solutions more urgent. ABC's chief meteorologist Ginger Zee found one possible answer. And I traveled to Mexico where many families struggle to access clean water.

5   High in the hills of Mexico, in the heart of the San Juan Kalchenko Forest, **1.** _____

_____ is a challenge at best.

We're heading to a small community outside of Mexico City to really witness firsthand the impact of the water crisis.

10   We wind our way around the Mexican mountainside, about 60 miles south of Mexico City, though it feels like a world away.

Guide: **2.** _____, to the Sasakanapa Spring.

L. Davis: And this spring has been around for?

15   *Guide:* Hundreds of years. And this is the closest spring to the community.

L. Davis: Tracing the steps of this tradition **3.** _____

_____.

Guide: It is right over here. But this is the travel that a person need to do.

L. Davis: Yeah, how do you do this if you have a lot of water?

20 *Guide:* Exactly, carrying a jug of water doing this, it is particularly hard.

L. Davis: Yeah. I can only imagine. It's hard enough without any water.

Guide: Right? And this is the spring. It's a tiny spring.

L. Davis: This has been a tradition for many of the villagers here for generations, where they make this trek, **4.** _____

25 _____, in order to get access to clean water from the sacred spring right here. And this water comes directly from the forest.

But as our Ginger Zee discovered, nearly 2,000 miles away, there are some viable solutions with new water-producing technology.

30 What might sound like a pipe dream is quickly becoming a reality.

C. Goddard, VP, Business Development North America, Source Global: Behind us is the first sourced hydropanel system here in Hinckley, California.

L. Davis: Safe drinking water **5.** _____.

35 *G. Zee, ABC News:* It's coming out. And I can just drink this right away?

C. Goddard: Totally.

G. Zee: Wow. It's hard for people to conceive of. You can make water from the water in the air?

C. Goddard: Absolutely. So, our team of researchers at Arizona State

40 University tried to say, how can we take the principles of renewable energy and apply it to drinking water? And what they developed

was the hydropanel, which uses a clever combination of a special material that absorbs hydrogen oxygen as well as a really clever thermodynamic process to convert [6.] _____

45 _____ into liquid drinking water without needing any power or water connections at all.

L. Davis: It's a fresh way to get safe drinking water in a community that cannot touch the groundwater. This hydropanel relies solely on the sun and the moisture in the air.

50 *G. Zee:* And then in its base is where it condenses and then it pumps up here.

C. Goddard: Yeah. Plug in these things anywhere. This is a fully off-grid, autonomous technology.

L. Davis: Hydropanels have brought drinking water to some of the most rural communities. A potentially life altering solution [7.] _____

55 _____.

An estimated two billion people, that's one in four around the world, do not have access to clean drinking water.

Notes   L. 7   **challenge at best**   「困難としか言いようがない」

L. 10   **wind our way around ~**   「~を曲がりくねって進みます」

L. 11   **world away**   「全く別世界」

L. 16   **Tracing the steps of ~**   「~の歩みをたどって登る」

L. 18   **But this is the travel that a person need to do.**   「But this is the travel that a person *needs* to do. 〈文法的には needs になる〉」

L. 24   **make this trek**   「この（険しい）道を歩む」

L. 31   **VP, Business Development North America, Source Global**   「北米事業開発部副社長, ソース・グローバル 〈VP= Vice President ソース・グローバル社は 2014 年設立のスタートアップ 企業で，世界の水道インフラがない地域を中心に幅広く事業を展開している〉」

L. 32   **sourced**   「導入した；提供した；調達した」

L. 32   **hydropanel system**   「ハイドロパネルシステム 〈太陽光発電パネルのような形状の飲料水生成 システム〉」

L. 32   **Hinckley**   「ヒンクリー 〈ロサンゼルスの北東に位置する街〉」

L. 40   **renewable energy**   「再生可能エネルギー」

L. 42   **clever combination**   「巧みな組み合わせ」

L. 43   **hydrogen oxygen**   「水素と酸素（の混合気体）」

L. 44   **thermodynamic process**   「熱力学的プロセス［過程］」

L. 48   **groundwater**   「地下水」

L. 51   **Plug in ~**   「~を差し込む；~をつなぐ」

L. 51   **off-grid**   「オフグリッドの；送電線網を利用しない」

L. 54   **life altering**   「（人々の）生活を変える［変えてしまう］ほどの」

Background of the News

　世界気象機関（WMO：World Meteorological Organization）が2021年10月に公表した予測によると，地球温暖化による気候変動，人口の増加や産業の発展などが影響し，2050年には世界で50億人が十分な水を確保できない状態に陥るという。2050年の世界人口は約100億人とされ，人類の2人に1人は水不足に苦しむことになる。そのため，水をめぐる対立や争いが懸念されている。このような世界的な水不足への対応として，安全な水を生成・確保する取り組みが広がっている。

　例えば，同じカリフォルニア州に本社を置く世界的IT企業セールスフォース社のフィスビルでは年間約780万ガロンに及ぶ廃水をろ過浄水できる設備を導入している。また，日本のベンチャー企業のWOTA株式会社は小型の浄水ボックスなどを開発しており，浄水設備としては非常にコンパクトであることが特徴で，2018年の西日本豪雨時における被災地支援にも役立った。

　これらのテクノロジーの導入により，水不足に苦しむ人々の生活を改善し，環境に負荷をかけない自己完結型の水供給システムの構築が目指されている。日本においても，地域によっては将来的な水不足の懸念が指摘されており，持続可能な水の供給は国連の持続可能な開発目標（SDGs）の一つとなっている。

▶ **After You Watch the News**　　*Exercises*

•)) **A** Listen to the news story and fill in the blanks in the text.

CD2-03 [Normal]　CD2-04 [Slow]

B Multiple Choice Questions: Select the best answer to each question.

1. According to the news story, the water crisis
   a. is only a challenge in poor areas of the world.
   b. is affecting 25 percent of the world's population.
   c. will soon be solved everywhere with new technology.

2. The water from the Sasakanapa Spring
   a. was recently discovered to be sacred.
   b. serves the people in the San Juan Kalchenko Forest and Mexico City.
   c. has been a community's source of clean drinking water for generations.

3. The hydropanel
   a. was invented by students at Arizona State University.
   b. uses the sun to convert vapor in the air to drinking water.
   c. uses a high-tech power source to draw water from the air.

4. Which statement is true regarding the current situation of hydropanels?
   a. They can be used anywhere.
   b. They are already helping people in most rural communities.
   c. Both *a* and *b*.

•)) C Translate the following Japanese into English. Then listen to the CD and practice the conversation with your partner. 🎧 DL 24 ◉ CD2-05

A: How was your year in Mexico?

B: It was really eye-opening. We take so much for granted here in the U.S.

A: What do you mean? The food? Entertainment?

B: Drinking water! **1.** _____

_____ .

A: **2.** _____ .

B: Really? I had no idea.

A: **3.** _____

_____ . They're turning to technology.

B: Let's hope for some good solutions!

1. 私が一緒に滞在した村人たちは，安全に飲める水を得るために何マイルも歩かなければなりませんでした。

2. きれいな飲み水を手に入れることは，ここでも一部の場所で問題になっています。

3. 地下水が飲めない辺ぴな地域はたくさんあります。

•)) **D** **Summary Practice:** Fill in the blanks with suitable words beginning with the letters indicated. Then listen to the CD and check your answers.

DL 25 CD2-06

The worldwide water (¹· c   ) is the focus of a special ABC World News series, taking its reporters from a mountainside in (²· M   ) to Hinckley, (³· C   ) to see firsthand some of the (⁴· s   ) being found. Linsey Davis joined a Mexican (⁵· g   ) on a (⁶· t   ) up steep hills to get drinking water from the Sasakanapa (⁷· S   )—a task that villagers have been forced to carry out for (⁸· g   ). Meanwhile, thousands of miles away in the U.S., Ginger Zee learned about an exciting new technology developed by (⁹· r   ) at Arizona State University which applies the principles of (¹⁰· r   ) (¹¹· e   ) to (¹²· d   ) water. Simply put, (¹³· h   ), as they are known, make water from (¹⁴· v   ) in the (¹⁵· a   ). They are proving to be a (¹⁶· v   ) solution to a worldwide problem affecting two (¹⁷· b   ) people. Off the grid, with no (¹⁸· p   ) or water source required, hydropanels could be the (¹⁹· l   ) (²⁰· a   ) solution many communities need.

E **Discussion:** Share your ideas and opinions with your classmates.

1. Look for updates on the use of hydropanels. Are they now widely in use? How have they been improved since this news story aired?

2. Is accessing safe water a challenge in Japan? If so, what is being done to provide clean drinking water to areas in need?

3. Look for information on another country that faces challenges to provide safe drinking water. Try to find out what strategies they are using to provide clean drinking water to people in need. Share your findings with the class.

waterの発音

　アメリカ英語ではwater /wɑtɚ, wɔːtɚ/は「ワァーラ」と聞こえることがある。これは前後を母音に挟まれた子音/t/を発音する際，本来の破裂音のように歯茎に舌先をつけて口腔内に息をためた後，開放するのではなくて，舌先を歯茎にすばやく弾いて発音されるので，日本語の「ラ」のように聞こえるためである。この/t/音は，前後を母音で挟まれている影響で有声音/d/になることもあるため，「ワァーダ」と聞こえることもある。

　また，centerは/n/音の後の/t/も舌先を歯茎にはじく音になったり，有声音/d/に変化したりするため，「センラー」や「センダー」のように聞こえる。

—We're heading to a small community outside of Mexico City to really witness firsthand the impact of the ***water*** crisis.　*(Safe Drinking Water, P. 49 L. 8)*

—Yeah, how do you do this if you have a lot of ***water***?　*(Safe Drinking Water, P. 49 L. 19)*

—…in order to get access to clean ***water*** from the sacred spring right here.

(Safe Drinking Water, P. 50 L. 25)

—…, there are some viable solutions with new ***water***-producing technology.

(Safe Drinking Water, P. 50 L. 28)

—You can make ***water*** from the ***water*** in the air?　*(Safe Drinking Water, P. 50 L. 37)*

—It's a fresh way to get safe drinking ***water*** in a community that cannot touch the ***groundwater***.　*(Safe Drinking Water, P. 51 L. 47)*

—Hydropanels have brought drinking ***water*** to some of the most rural communities.

(Safe Drinking Water, P. 51 L. 53)

—…, reaching out to residents impacted by that train derailment that spewed toxic chemicals into the air and ***water***…　*(Increased Outreach in East Palestine, P. 96 L. 3)*

—So far, more than two million gallons of contaminated ***water*** pumped away.

(Increased Outreach in East Palestine, P. 97 L. 25)

—From the beginning, students have been front and ***center***.　*(Honoring Earth Day, P. 9 L. 5)*

—He always made sure that everybody had a toy in the cancer ***center***.

(David's Toy Project, P. 44 L. 8)

Students Create Prosthesis for Dog

The Gist
- What happened to the teacher's dog Bentley?
- How were the students able to help him?

▶ **Before You Watch the News**   *Warm-up Exercises*

•)) **A** **Vocabulary Check:** Choose the correct definition for each of the words below.

🎧 DL 26   ⊙ CD2-07

1. diagnose   (   )   a. physical; something that can be touched
2. amputate   (   )   b. to inspire someone to do something
3. prototype   (   )   c. to cut off a limb using a surgical operation
4. tangible   (   )   d. a preliminary model of something
5. compel   (   )   e. to identify an illness by examining the symptoms

B Fill in the blanks with appropriate expressions from the Vocabulary Check above. Change the word forms where necessary.

1. A (   ) of the new drone is expected to be released early next year.
2. I want to believe what you're saying, Curt, but we need (   ) evidence that Scott was at the scene of the crime.
3. So many friends recommended that book that I felt (   ) to read it myself.
4. Ben learned to walk with crutches after his leg was (   ).
5. When she was (   ) with pneumonia, Lila was instructed to get plenty of bed rest and to take her medication three times a day.

D. Muir: Finally tonight here, the teacher, her dog, and the students who were determined to do something. But what they've done is "America Strong."

Tonight, in Charlotte, North Carolina, the high school students at Providence Day School on a mission to help their teacher and her beloved dog. Everyone at school knows Bentley, their math teacher Ms. Ashley Liberto's golden retriever. [1.] _____ _____, Bentley was diagnosed with cancer and had to have his front right leg amputated. It didn't stop Bentley, slowly recovering, relearning to walk, swim, to play fetch.

A. Liberto, teacher: Still has it.

D. Muir: But [2.] _____.

B. Hollis, student: David, we'd like you to meet Bentley.

D. Muir: Mr. Todd Johnson's computer science class getting to work.

T. Johnson, teacher: Hi, David.

D. Muir: Mr. Johnson.

T. Johnson: [3.] _____ in finding a way to get Bentley a little more mobile. Um, you know, I knew my students were up to the challenge.

D. Muir: The students began building a prosthetic leg. Their designs coming to life on the 3D printer, holding the prototypes. Bentley arriving at

school, getting fitted for his new leg.

A. Liberto: This is a good one.

D. Muir: The students measuring, **4.** _____.

25   Senior Brandon Hollis.

B. Hollis: Knowing that this project would have this real-world, tangible impact on a life is what really compelled me.

D. Muir: Junior Houston Dee.

H.Dee, student: Sometimes, you just got to go for it. You've got to find

30   something that you're passionate about and **5.** _____

        _____.

D. Muir: And this evening, just look at Bentley. His first steps in their newest design. And right here, tonight...

A. Liberto: Hey, David.

35 **D. Muir:** Their teacher, Ms. Liberto, and her Bentley.

A. Liberto: My reaction when the students came up with the design was just,

        6. _____ and so touched by them.

D. Muir: Tonight, the students coming together for their teacher and her dog.

Everyone: Bye, David.

40 **D. Muir:** And Bentley coming right to the camera, there. Go, Bentley and those incredible students. We hope, of course, this is the first of many of their inventions ahead. I'm David Muir. I'll see you right back here, tomorrow. Good night.

Notes   L. 5   **Providence Day School**   「プロビデンス・デイ・スクール〈ノースカロライナ州シャーロット市にある私立高校で，男女共学の進学校〉」

L. 10   **play fetch**   「ボール遊び；取ってこい遊び〈ボールなどを投げて、犬に取りに行かせる遊び。fetch は行って取ってくること〉」

L. 11   **Still has it**   「まだやれるわ〈ガンで足の切断を経験したにもかかわらず，彼はまだ元気な昔のままだ〉」

L. 14   **getting to work**   「（義足作りの）作業を始めた」

L. 18   **were up to the challenge**   「挑戦に取り組める；チャレンジしてくれる」

L. 22   **getting fitted for ~**   「~の調整を受ける」

L. 29   **go for it**   「（とにかく）やってみる；目標に向かって進む［努力する］；頑張る」

▶ **After You Watch the News** **Exercises**

•)) **A** Listen to the news story and fill in the blanks in the text.

CD2-08 [Normal]   CD2-09 [Slow]

B **Multiple Choice Questions:** Select the best answer to each question.

1. The students decided to help Ms. Liberto's dog
   a. because they loved the dog so much.
   b. because it was an assignment for class.
   c. in order to prevent his cancer from returning.

2. Which of the following statements is true regarding the students at Providence Day School?
   a. They decided to help the teacher's dog in their computer science class.
   b. They were unable to find a way to make a tangible impact using their invention.
   c. They found a way to make the dog more mobile without any of their teachers knowing.

3. The students succeeded in making the prosthetic leg
   a. with the first carefully-designed prototype.
   b. after readjusting the design numerous times.
   c. using information they learned in Ms. Liberto's math class.

4. Bentley the dog

    a. learned to walk again even before getting the prosthetic leg.

    b. gained increased mobility when the prosthetic leg was fitted.

    c. Both *a* and *b*.

•)) C Translate the following Japanese into English. Then listen to the CD and practice the conversation with your partner.   🎧 DL 27   ◉ CD2-10

A: Are you boys still here? Class ended an hour ago. What are you doing?

B: [1.] Ms. Liberto is bringing Bentley to school tomorrow so _____

_____.

C: We measured really carefully this time. [2.] _____

_____.

A: Okay! Put it right there and let's see what happens.

B: Wow! This one looks perfect.

A: I'm so proud of you boys. I know this is a real mission for you.

C: It is! [3.] _____

_____.

1. リベルト先生が明日ベントレーを学校に連れてくるので、もう１つ試作品を作ってみたいのです。
2. もう３Ｄプリンターのための準備はできたと思います。
3. 私たちはベントレーの生活に影響を与えるようなことをしているのです。

•)) **D** **Summary Practice:** Fill in the blanks with suitable words beginning with the letters indicated. Then listen to the CD and check your answers.

DL 28   CD2-11

Bentley, the beloved pet of (1. **m**   ) teacher Ashley Liberto, had to have one of his legs (2. **a**   ) after being (3. **d**   ) with (4. **c**   ). The (5. **g**   ) (6. **r**   ) eventually regained the ability to (7. **w**   ) and (8. **s**   ), but Ms. Liberto hoped for him to become more (9. **m**   ). Todd Johnson and his (10. **c**   ) (11. **s**   ) class came to the rescue. The students created (12. **p**   ) on the school's 3D (13. **p**   ), making adjustments until they got it just right. Their determination paid off, and Bentley was fitted with a new (14. **p**   ) (15. **l**   ). Ms. Liberto was so (16. **t**   ) that the students were able to come up with a (17. **d**   ) that worked. For the students at Providence Day School, the project offered a chance to do something they felt (18. **p**   ) about. And for Bentley—well, there's no stopping him now!

E **Discussion:** Share your ideas and opinions with your classmates.

1. How much do you know about prosthetics? What body parts can be replaced? Do an internet search and see what you can find out. Share your finding with the class.

2. Look for other news stories about animals. Share your findings with your classmates.

Inside ChatGPT Technology

The Gist
- What is ChatGPT?
- How is it apt to influence our lives?

▶ **Before You Watch the News**   *Warm-up Exercises*

•)) **A Vocabulary Check:** Choose the correct definition for each of the words below.

🎧 DL 29   💿 CD2-12

1. unveil   (   )   a. possibility
2. exhilarating (   )   b. thrilling; exciting
3. potential   (   )   c. to remove; to get rid of
4. integrate   (   )   d. to show or reveal
5. eliminate   (   )   e. to join or combine

B Fill in the blanks with appropriate expressions from the Vocabulary Check above. Change the word forms where necessary.

1. I love Prof. Lin's classes. She always manages to (   ) culture into the language program.
2. The new statue in the town square will be (   ) at today's ceremony.
3. Unfortunately, our ice hockey team was (   ) in the first round.
4. This is my first time to visit France. Just being in Paris is so (   )!
5. Mark has a lot of (   ). Law school is not out of the question if he studies harder next year.

D. Muir: Now to the ABC News exclusive tonight. We take you inside the company called OpenAI, artificial intelligence, their new technology, GPT-4. And even if you haven't heard of it, how it could soon affect your life. Tonight, what that technology can now do, from passing the bar exam to answering SAT questions. Here's our chief business correspondent Rebecca Jarvis.

R. Jarvis: Tonight, we take you inside the headquarters of a small company in San Francisco called OpenAI, creators of ChatGPT. Even if you haven't heard of it, [1.] _____

_____ by this powerful new technology built with artificial intelligence. Just this week, OpenAI unveiling its newest version, which can answer complex questions in seconds. It can write speeches, take tests. We learned it can now even pass the bar exam to become a lawyer, placing in the top 10 percent. They believe it could one day help doctors spot disease that the human eye or mind might miss. The CEO, Sam Altman, is just 37.

What changes because of artificial intelligence?

S. Altman, CEO, OpenAI: Part of the exciting thing here is we... we get continually surprised by the creative power of... of all of society.

R. Jarvis: I think that word surprised, though, it's both exhilarating as well as terrifying for people.

S. Altman: That's for sure. ^{2.} _____

that we're a little bit scared of this, I think people should be happy.

R. Jarvis: You're a little bit scared?

25 *S. Altman:* A little bit, yeah, of course.

R. Jarvis: You personally?

S. Altman: I think if I said I were not, you should either not trust me or be very unhappy I'm in this job.

R. Jarvis: Concerned because they acknowledge even ^{3.} _____

30 _____ of what they've created. OpenAI's chief technology officer, Mira Murati, shows us the new version out this week. Just listen as I ask a complicated SAT question.

Lisa gives her brother Sam a 15-second head start in a 300-meter
35 *race. During the race, Sam runs at an average speed of five meters per second. Lisa runs at an average speed of eight meters per second, not including the head start. Since the last time Lisa started running, which of the following best approximates the number of seconds that had passed when Lisa caught up to Sam?*

40 Within seconds, it answers correctly. The answer is B, 25 seconds. And so, we pressed about the potential for cheating.

You have this, ^{4.} _____

_____ at the SATs, the bar exam. How should schools be integrating this technology in a way that doesn't increase

45   cheating, that doesn't increase laziness among students?

S. Altman: Education is going to have to change, uhm, but it's happened many other times with technology. When we got the calculator, the way we taught math and what we tested students on, that totally changed. The, the promise of this technology, one of the ones that
50   **5.** _____ is the ability to provide individual learning, great individual learning for each student.

R. Jarvis: They argue the eventual benefits outweigh the negatives.

You've said AI will likely eliminate millions of jobs. Many people are
55   gonna ask, why on earth did you create this technology?

S. Altman: I think it can do the opposite of all of those things, too. It is going to eliminate a lot of current jobs. That's true. We can make much better ones. The reason to develop AI at all is that I... I believe this will be, ah, in terms of impact on our lives and improving our lives,
60   an upside. This will be the greatest technology humanity has yet developed.

R. Jarvis: So, in the wrong human hands, it could be a very different device. It could be a very different power.

S. Altman: We do worry a lot about authoritarian governments developing
65   this and using this for...

R. Jarvis: Russia. China. Are you speaking to the government?

S. Altman: Oh, yes.

R. Jarvis: You're in regular contact?

S. Altman: Regular contact.

70 *R. Jarvis:* And do you think they get it?

S. Altman: More and more every day.

D. Muir: That is really something. **6.** _____
_____ of this
artificial intelligence. And it would seem they're trying to sound the

alarm to the U.S. government about Russia and China wanting to get their hands on this, because it's here. Have they talked to the Biden administration about this?

R. Jarvis: David, Sam Altman tells me they're in consistent contact and that the reason here is that this is an AI arms race. Everybody wants this technology. ^{7.}_____ _____ has huge control over our future and our lives.

Notes
 L. 1 **Now to ~** 「さて（次は），～をお伝えします」
 L. 3 **GPT-4** 「ジーピーティー・フォー〈＝ Generative Pre-trained Transformer 4 OpenAI 社が 2023 年 3 月にリリースした大規模言語モデル。テキストと画像の両方の入力を受け入れて情報の処理・出力ができるマルチモーダルモデルで，高度な推理機能を持っており，人間と変わらないような流暢な言語出力ができるという〉」
 L. 5 **bar exam** 「司法試験」
 L. 5 **SAT** 「大学進学適性試験〈＝ Scholastic Assessment Test アメリカの大学受験のための統一標準テストで，多くの大学で受験の際，受けることを義務付けている〉」
 L. 5 **chief business correspondent** 「ビジネス担当主任記者［リポーター］」
 L.31 **chief technology officer** 「最高技術責任者〈IT 関連の企業を中心に使用されている役職名で，技術面や研究開発を監督する。略語は CTO〉」
 L.34 **head start** 「優先スタート〈陸上レースなどで競走相手より早くスタートすること〉」
 L.41 **pressed about ~** 「～について質問した；～について回答を求めた」
 L.51 **individual learning** 「個別学習；個人的学習」
 L.64 **authoritarian governments** 「独裁主義政権」
 L.72 **something** 「すごいこと；素晴らしいこと」
 L.79 **AI arms race** 「AI をめぐる激しい競争〈arms race は軍拡競争の意味で，AI arms race という表現には，AI が他の兵器同様，人類に脅威をもたらす恐れがあるものだという意味合いが込められている〉」

Background of the News

　2023年7月2日付の『産経新聞』によると，欧州連合（EU）欧州議会は，対話型人工知能（AI: artificial intelligence）である「チャットGPT」を含む生成AIの活用に対する規制強化の動きを進めており，世界的に規制づくりの動きが加速している。AIの活用によって著作権の侵害や偽情報の拡散リスクが指摘されているものの，AIの活用範囲は広がりつつある。

　実際，生成AIは欧米の弁護士や会計士の業界で活用されつつあり，就職活動の対策に利用する学生も徐々に増えている。また，米金融大手ゴールドマン・サックスによる分析では，AIの自然言語処理技術が世界の国内総生産（GDP）を7％増加させ，生産性の伸びを1.5ポイント押し上げる可能性があるとされている。

　AIの普及により，何百万もの雇用（millions of jobs）が失われる可能性も指摘されている。さらに，チャットGPTは学習のために大量の情報を取り込む。そのため，個人情報を違法に集める潜在的な危険性（potential dangers）にも懸念が寄せられ，アメリカでは利用者がオープンAI社を提訴する事例も発生している。

　しかし，同社の最高経営責任者（CEO）であるサム・アルトマン（Sam Altman）が言うように，すべてのテクノロジーにはリスクと恩恵（benefits）がある。世界にとって，今後この技術がより多くの恩恵をもたらすことを期待したい。

► **After You Watch the News**　　*Exercises*

•)) **A** Listen to the news story and fill in the blanks in the text.

CD2-13 [Normal]　　CD2-14 [Slow]

B **Multiple Choice Questions:** Select the best answer to each question.

1. Which of the following statements is true concerning ChatGPT?
   a. Some people worry about Russia and China getting this technology.
   b. It is expected to help the U.S. win the arms race with Russia and China.
   c. It was developed through consistent contact with Russian and Chinese tech companies.

2. What is the expected impact of ChatGPT?
   a. It will create new and better jobs.
   b. It will provide more opportunities for students to take the SATs and the bar exam.
   c. Both *a* and *b*.

3. Sam Altman
    a. is exhilarated but also scared that AI cannot be trusted.
    b. insists that even in the wrong hands, AI will help to improve our lives in many ways.
    c. believes that education will have to change, but that AI can help individual learning.

4. According to the news story, which of the following is a possible use of AI?
    a. It can beat most humans on complicated tests, but sometimes cheats.
    b. It could potentially assist doctors to detect diseases that humans miss.
    c. It could help authoritarian governments to better communicate with the U.S.

•)) C Translate the following Japanese into English. Then listen to the CD and practice the conversation with your partner.　　　　🎧 DL 30　◎ CD2-15

A: Have you heard about that new ChatGPT?
B: Yeah! It's pretty exciting, don't you think?
A: Exciting? Not really. 1. _____.
B: Well, it's up to teachers like us to do something about it.
A: Like what? 2. _____

_____.

B: 3. But _____

_____.

A: Well frankly, I'm scared.
B: Come on! People should be happy about these advances.

1. 私はカンニングの可能性が心配です。
2. この新しいテクノロジーについては，学生の方が私たちよりずっと詳しいのです。
3. でも，私たちの学生が怠けないように，このテクノロジーを取り入れる方法を見つけるのは私たちの責任です。

•)) **D** **Summary Practice:** Fill in the blanks with suitable words beginning with the letters indicated. Then listen to the CD and check your answers.

DL 31   CD2-16

Sam Altman, the 37-year-old CEO of the (¹·**c**   ) that created (²·**C**   ), sat down with ABC News for an exclusive talk about what to expect from this new (³·**t**   ). According to Altman, although they don't yet know its full (⁴·**p**   ), (⁵·**a**   ) (⁶·**i**   ) will impact our daily lives in many ways. The newest (⁷·**v**   ), recently (⁸·**u**   ) by San Francisco-based OpenAI, is able to answer (⁹·**c**   ) test questions from the SATs and (¹⁰·**b**   ) (¹¹·**e**   ) in just (¹²·**s**   ). Its creators are hopeful that it will eventually also help (¹³·**d**   ) detect (¹⁴·**d**   ) that humans can't spot. ABC's Rebecca Jarvis says all of this is both (¹⁵·**e**   ) and (¹⁶·**t**   ). Altman, however, insists that with schools (¹⁷·**i**   ) this new technology and regular communication with the (¹⁸·**g**   ), developing AI will (¹⁹·**i**   ) our (²⁰·**l**   ).

E **Discussion:** Share your ideas and opinions with your classmates.

1. As this news story suggests, there are both benefits and potentially negative aspects of the rapid development of artificial intelligence. In addition to educational issues, what are other areas of concern?

2. Sam Altman claims that AI "will be the greatest technology humanity has yet developed." Do you agree with him? Why or why not?

3. How has ChatGPT impacted your life and the lives of those around you? Share your answers with your classmates.

縮約形の多用

　書き言葉を媒体とした英字新聞やオンラインのニュース記事とは異なって，テレビニュースで使われる英語の場合は縮約形が多用される。ニュースキャスターやリポーターがthey've, it's, isn't, can't, she'sなどの縮約形を使用することで，口語体のくだけた調子を表現している。

—…of what *they've* created.　　　　　　　　　　*(ChatGPT Technology, P. 64 L. 30)*

—But what *they've* done is "America Strong."

(Students Create Prosthesis for Dog, P. 57 L. 2)

—And even if you *haven't* heard of it, how it could soon affect your life.

(ChatGPT Technology, P. 63 L. 3)

—I think that word surprised, though, *it's* both exhilarating as well as

terrifying for people.　　　　　　　　　　　*(ChatGPT Technology, P. 63 L. 20)*

—…Russia and China wanting to get their hands on this, because *it's* here.

(ChatGPT Technology, P. 66 L. 75)

—*It's* becoming more dire, and the search for solutions more urgent.

(Safe Drinking Water, P. 49 L. 1)

—*It's* a fresh way to get safe drinking water in a community…

(Safe Drinking Water, P. 51 L. 47)

—At its peak, *it's* estimated *it'll* produce 180,000 barrels of oil per day, …

(Drilling Project in Alaska, P. 84 L. 13)

—*She's* one of America's most beloved college basketball fans.

(Sister Jean, the Beloved Chaplain, P. 72 L. 3)

Air Date: February 18, 2023
Duration: 1' 38"

Sister Jean, the Beloved Chaplain

The Gist
- Who is Sister Jean, and why is she in the news?
- What do her students say about her?

▶ **Before You Watch the News** | *Warm-up Exercises*

•)) **A Vocabulary Check:** Choose the correct definition for each of the words below.

🎧 DL 32   ◉ CD2-17

1.	chaplain	( )	a.	encouragement; support
2.	sensation	( )	b.	a clergy member affiliated with a particular institution
3.	boost	( )	c.	a person or product that causes great excitement
4.	embodiment	( )	d.	a visible form of a particular quality
5.	calling	( )	e.	vocation; the urge to pursue a certain career

B Fill in the blanks with appropriate expressions from the Vocabulary Check above. Change the word forms where necessary.

1. Sarah has been depressed since her cat ran away. Your visit will give her a real ( ).

2. After spending five years in London, Ted is the ( ) of British style.

3. Those designer boots are selling so fast! They're a real ( )!

4. My cousin was just appointed ( ) at the state prison.

5. Dave always knew he'd become a doctor. He says he had a special ( ).

W. Johnson: Finally, tonight, "America Strong." Sister Jean, the beloved chaplain, sharing her incredible story.

She's one of America's most beloved college basketball fans. Sister Jean Dolores Schmidt, chaplain for the Loyola University men's
5   basketball team in Chicago.

Sports commentator: Time-out. They don't take it.

W. Johnson: Becoming an international sensation during the 2018 NCAA tournament when her Ramblers [1.]_____
_____. At 103, Sister Jean is still on the job.

10 *Sister Jean, Chaplain, Loyola Ramblers men's basketball team:* I sit here so that I don't get hit with the ball.

Basketball player: Her presence is something that is felt every single day and it's awesome. And it makes the players just have that little extra boost of confidence.

15 *W. Johnson:* And still [2.]_____.

Student: Everyone loves Sister Jean. There's not a single unkind bone in her body, and she represents our values and, like, she's the embodiment of compassion.

W. Johnson: Now, Sister Jean is sharing her wisdom on faith and basketball
20   with a memoir to be published [3.]_____.

Her dream of becoming a sister and a teacher began early.

Sister Jean: My dream started when I was in third grade.

W. Johnson: She followed her calling and, for nearly 30 years, has been working primarily with student basketball players.

25 *Sister Jean:* I think sports are very important because ^{4.} _____ _____. And during those life skills, you're also talking about faith and purpose.

W. Johnson: A lifetime of service, and her mission continues.

Sister Jean: I want them to be happy people.

30 *W. Johnson:* Sister Jean, ^{5.} _____. I'm Whit Johnson in New York. Good night.

Notes
L. 4 **Loyola University** 「ロヨラ大学〈シカゴ市内にある 1870 年創立の大規模私立大学〉」
L. 5 **Chicago** 「シカゴ〈イリノイ州北東部，ミシガン湖岸に位置する同州最大の都市〉」
L. 7 **NCAA** 「= National Collegiate Athletic Association 米大学体育協会」
L. 8 **Ramblers** 「ランブラーズ〈ここではロヨラ大学の男子バスケットボールチームを指す。The Loyola Ramblers もしくは Loyola Chicago Ramblers と呼ばれる〉」
L. 9 **still on the job** 「まだ現役；今でもその仕事に取り組んでいる」
L. 16 **not a single unkind bone in her body** 「不親切なところが何もない；親切そのもの〈not have a ... bone in one's body が基本のパターンで使われ，例えば have a bad bone in one's body で（生まれつき）性格が悪いという意味になる。bone は人の性質や本質を表す〉」
L. 18 **compassion** 「思いやり」
L. 20 **memoir** 「自伝；回顧録」
L. 28 **lifetime of service** 「生涯にわたる奉仕；生涯現役」

•)) **A** Listen to the news story and fill in the blanks in the text.

○ CD2-18 [Normal]　○ CD2-19 [Slow]

B **Multiple Choice Questions:** select the best answer to each question.

1. The Loyola Ramblers
   a. have become an international sensation.
   b. are influenced every day by Sister Jean.
   c. were the winners of the 2018 NCAA tournament.

2. According to the news story, Sister Jean
   a. coaches a college basketball team.
   b. will retire after writing her memoir.
   c. has been working with basketball players for decades.

3. Sister Jean's dream
   a. was really to play basketball.
   b. was different from her calling.
   c. began when she was a young child.

4. According to a student, Sister Jean helps their basketball team to
   a. become more confident.
   b. develop their basketball techniques.
   c. find their own calling as athletes or chaplains.

•)) **C** Translate the following Japanese into English. Then listen to the CD and practice the conversation with your partner.　　🎧 DL 33　○ CD2-20

A: Sister Jean, why did you decide to become a chaplain?

B: ¹·Students ask me that question a lot and _____

_____.

A: How old were you when you knew?

B: ²·Well actually, _____

_____.

A: Why basketball, Sister? Couldn't you just work at a church?

B: [3.]I always believed that _____

_____.

A: That's enough questions for now. Anyhow, we're so glad you're here, Sister Jean!

1. 学生たちからよく聞かれる質問ですが，私はいつも，天職だったと答えています。

2. 実は，私の夢はずっと前の3年生のときに始まったのです。

3. スポーツは，人生のスキルや信念や目標などについて話す機会を与えてくれると，いつも信じていたからです。

•)) **D** **Summary Practice:** Fill in the blanks with suitable words beginning with the letters indicated. Then listen to the CD and check your answers.

🎧 DL 34   ◉ CD2-21

Sister Jean Dolores Schmidt, or simply "Sister Jean," as she is affectionately known, is the adored ([1.]**c** _____) of the Loyola University men's ([2.]**b** _____) ([3.]**t** _____), the ([4.]**R** _____). Now 103, she became a worldwide ([5.]**s** _____) back in 2018 during the NCAA ([6.]**t** _____) when her team placed in the ([7.]**f** _____) ([8.]**f** _____). Sister Jean, who says her ([9.]**c** _____) started back in third grade, has been working ([10.]**p** _____) with students who play basketball for nearly ([11.]**t** _____) years. According to her students, she is the ([12.]**e** _____) of ([13.]**c** _____) and gives them a ([14.]**b** _____) of ([15.]**c** _____). We all look forward to reading her ([16.]**m** _____), due out soon.

E **Discussion:** Share your ideas and opinions with your classmates.

1. Is there a sports team at your university or in your city that you support? Do they have someone like Sister Jean who supports and motivates them? Do they have special team colors or a team mascot to create a sense of spirit and excite their fans? Share your answers with your classmates.

2. Look for other stories about senior citizens who are actively engaged with young people. What kind of contributions are they making to society?

Air Date: May 24, 2023
Duration: 2'13"

Paralyzed Man Walks Again

The Gist
- What kind of progress is being made in dealing with spinal cord injuries?
- What is the current situation of Gert-Jan Oskam?

▶ **Before You Watch the News** | ***Warm-up Exercises***

•)) **A** **Vocabulary Check:** Choose the correct definition for each of the words below.

🎧 DL 35　　◉ CD2-22

1. breakthrough　(　)　**a.** innovation; advance
2. groundbreaking　(　)　**b.** to go around; to circumvent
3. stimulate　(　)　**c.** to energize; to revitalize
4. bypass　(　)　**d.** pioneering; revolutionary
5. beacon　(　)　**e.** shining example or source of encouragement

B Fill in the blanks with appropriate expressions from the Vocabulary Check above. Change the word forms where necessary.

1. We need to find a better way to (　　　) sales if we want to remain competitive.
2. John is nearly 80, but he's still a (　　　) of light to the community.
3. That company has just announced a (　　　) in their search for drugs effective against Alzheimer's Disease.
4. Tom's team is doing (　　　) research on gene therapy.
5. Slow down! If we try to (　　　) too many steps, our experiment won't work.

D. Muir: We turn now to the remarkable medical breakthrough tonight when it comes to spinal cord injuries. Groundbreaking technology helping a paralyzed man walk again for the first time in more than a decade. Implants in the brain and the spinal cord, **1.** _____

5 _____ to walk again, to climb stairs. Will Reeve tonight on what this could mean.

W. Reeve: Tonight, groundbreaking new technology enabling a paralyzed man to walk again for the first time in more than a decade, thanks in part to the power of his own thoughts. Gert-Jan Oskam was

10 **2.** _____ .

G-J Oskam, patient: Twelve years ago, I got in an accident and had a spinal cord injury. So, **3.** _____

_____ .

W. Reeve: A year ago, scientists in Switzerland placing electronic implants in

15 areas of his brain and spinal cord that control movement. Then, using artificial intelligence, researchers building what they call a digital bridge, establishing a wireless connection between Oskam's brain and spinal cord to stimulate movement, bypassing the injured areas of his body, essentially **4.** _____

20 _____ .

G-J Oskam: I could control my hips. The brain implants picked up what I was doing with my hips.

W. Reeve: The 40-year-old has been able to stand, walk, and even climb stairs with the help of those implants. And even when the implants are turned off, Oskam [5.] _____

_____. The researcher saying, he developed new nerve connections.

Dr. J. Bloch, Swiss Federal Institute of Technology Lausanne: We can give back hope to the people with the spinal cord injury and they will be able to walk again thanks to the digital bridge.

D. Muir: This is really just incredible. Will Reeve with us tonight. And, Will, I know that whenever there's news on spinal cord injuries, any new hope or potential breakthroughs, that this is really personal for you and your family.

W. Reeve: Yeah, David. My father Christopher Reeve was, in many ways, the face of paralysis after his spinal cord injury in 1995. And he dreamed of breakthroughs like this, and he fought for them. He would've been the first person to volunteer for this procedure. It still is early days. The treatment is not yet widely available to patients, but this provides a bright beacon of hope for the spinal cord injury community, David.

D. Muir: And [6.] _____

_____, Will, that you're reporting on these breakthroughs. Will Reeve tonight. Will, thank you.

Notes   L. 2   **spinal cord injuries** 「脊髄損傷」
         L. 4   **Implants** 「インプラント；機器を体内に埋め込むこと」
         L. 14   **electronic implants** 「電子インプラント」
         L. 16   **artificial intelligence** 「人工知能；AI」
         L. 17   **digital bridge** 「デジタルブリッジ〈脳と脊髄の間をワイヤレス接続すること〉」
         L. 21   **picked up ~** 「読み取った」
         L. 27   **nerve connections** 「神経細胞の結合［接続］〈脊髄内で新たに神経接続が起きた〉」
         L. 28   **Swiss Federal Institute of Technology Lausanne** 「スイス連邦工科大学ローザンヌ校」
         L. 35   **Christopher Reeve** 「クリストファー・リーブ〈映画「スーパーマン」シリーズのスーパーマン役俳優として有名。事故で脊髄損傷を起こし，首から下が麻痺する怪我を負った〉」
         L. 38   **procedure** 「治療法；手術」

 After You Watch the News   *Exercises*

•)) **A** Listen to the news story and fill in the blanks in the text.

 CD2-23 [Normal]   CD2-24 [Slow]

B **Multiple Choice Questions:** select the best answer to each question.

1. Gert-Jan Oskam's treatment is described as "groundbreaking" because
   a. it was carried out by a team of robots.
   b. it involves a totally new kind of AI technology.
   c. Oskam had not been able to walk for over ten years.

2. Oskam's electronic implants
   a. were placed in the injured areas of his body.
   b. are in areas of the body that control movement.
   c. cannot be turned on and off.

3. The digital bridge designed by researchers
   a. sends signals from Oskam's brain to his hips.
   b. involved inserting a thin wire into Oskam's brain.
   c. connects Oskam's spinal cord and his legs wirelessly.

4. Will Reeve
   a. became the face of spinal cord injuries after he had an accident.
   b. is a bright beacon of hope for the spinal cord injury community.
   c. had a close family member who suffered from a spinal cord injury.

•)) **C** Translate the following Japanese into English. Then listen to the CD and practice the conversation with your partner. 🎧 DL 36 💿 CD2-25

    A: Did you hear the news about Gert-Jan?

    B: ^{1.}I heard _____

        _____. What happened?

    A: Well, with the implants, he can walk again! And he can even climb stairs!

    B: That's incredible! ^{2.}_____. How did they do it?

    A: ^{3.}I don't really understand the details, but it seems _____

        _____

        _____.

    B: So you mean his body could read his thoughts?

    A: Something like that. It's amazing, isn't it?

    1. 彼は画期的な新技術を試すためにスイスに行ったと聞きました。

    2. 彼は10年以上も体が麻痺していました。

    3. 詳細はよく分からないのですが，医師たちはAI技術を使って彼の脳と脊髄の間につながりを築くことができたようです。

•)) **D** **Summary Practice:** Fill in the blanks with suitable words beginning with the letters indicated. Then listen to the CD and check your answers.

🎧 DL 37 💿 CD2-26

AI is in the news tonight in an incredible story of a medical (^{1.}**b**   ) aided by (^{2.}**t**   ). Gert-Jan Oskam, now (^{3.}**f**   ), was involved in a serious (^{4.}**m**   ) accident twelve years ago, leaving him (^{5.}**p**   ). A team of (^{6.}**s**   ) in (^{7.}**S**   ) developed a (^{8.}**g**   ) solution involving placing (^{9.}**i**   ) in Oskam's (^{10.}**b**   ) and spinal cord that enabled him to control his (^{11.}**h**   ). How were they able to do that? By using (^{12.}**a**   ) (^{13.}**i**   ) to create a (^{14.}**w**   ) connection called a digital (^{15.}**b**   ). Will Reeve, whose famous father also suffered from a spinal cord injury, reports that the bridge successfully enabled Oskam to (^{16.}**s**   ), walk and (^{17.}**c**   ) (^{18.}**s**   ). Though not yet widely available, this amazing treatment is a (^{19.}**b**   ) of hope for the spinal cord injury (^{20.}**c**   ).

E **Discussion:** Share your ideas and opinions with your classmates.

1. With the uses of AI technology rapidly expanding, its good and bad sides are the topic of much debate. With your classmates, brainstorm some of the positive and potentially negative uses of AI. Do you think the government should introduce strict regulations? Why or why not?

2. Gert-Jan Oskam became paralyzed due to a motorcycle accident. Will Reeve's father, Christopher Reeve, was also paralyzed with a spinal cord injury. See if you can find out what caused it, and why people were so interested in Mr. Reeve's case.

3. Look for other medical news stories that could give people hope. Share them with your classmates.

子音[h]と[ð]の脱落

　助動詞have, has, hadや人称代名詞のhe, him, his, herなどの語頭の子音/h/は，強調して発音する場合を除き，脱落して発音されないことが多い。例えば，have /həv/は/h/が脱落して/əv/になることがある。また，短縮形が使われたり話すスピードがさらに速くなったりすると，/v/も脱落してあいまい母音の/ə/しか残らないこともある。以下の一つ目の例では短縮形のwould've /wʊdəv/が「ウッダ(ブ)」と聞こえる。

—He ***would've*** been the first person to volunteer for this procedure.

(Paralyzed Man Walks Again, P. 78 L. 37)

—... breakthroughs like this, and ***he*** fought for them.

(Paralyzed Man Walks Again, P. 78 L. 37)

　また，them /ðəm/ の/ð/音も脱落しやすい。以下の例ではwant の/t/音とthemの/ð/音が脱落して聞こえにくくなっているためwant them /wan(tð)əm/「ワンネム」のように聞こえる。

—I ***want them*** to be happy people.　　(Sister Jean, the Beloved Chaplain, P. 73 L. 29)

　同様に，次の例ではandの/d/音とthenの/ð/音が弱くなっているので，and then /ən(dð)en/「エンネン」のように聞こえる。このように，語末とその次に続く単語の頭の発音が同じ(似ている)とき，子音は脱落しやすい。

—***And then*** in its base is where it condenses and then it pumps up here.

(Safe Drinking Water, P. 51 L. 50)

—Nope, I ***paid them***, I... because that's how I was raised.

(Student Loan Showdown, P. 15 L. 26)

—Hundreds ***have been*** arrested...　　　　　　　　(Fury in France, P. 90 L. 4)

—Garbage collectors ***have been*** on strike for 13 days now.　　(Fury in France, P. 90 L. 17)

—I'm pleased that there ***have been*** no exceedances for residential air quality
　standards...　　　　　　　　(Increased Outreach in East Palestine, P. 96 L. 10)

Air Date: March 13, 2023
Duration: 1'46"

Drilling Project in Alaska

The Gist
■ What kind of drilling project has been proposed by the president?
■ Why is the project controversial?

▶ **Before You Watch the News** | *Warm-up Exercises*

•)) **A Vocabulary Check:** Choose the correct definition for each of the words below.

🎧 DL 38   ⦿ CD2-27

1.	generate	( )	a.	to reverse; to abolish
2.	peak	( )	b.	to produce; to bring about
3.	renege	( )	c.	maximum; highest point
4.	compromise	( )	d.	to go back on one's promise
5.	overturn	( )	e.	an agreement in which each side makes concessions

B Fill in the blanks with appropriate expressions from the Vocabulary Check above. Change the word forms where necessary.

1. If the findings of Tom's research project are (   ), he's apt to leave the university.
2. If you and Sam are unable to reach a (   ), the deal is off.
3. Car sales reached an all-time (   ) when Lee was put in charge.
4. Winning the state championship (   ) a great deal of publicity for the school's sports program.
5. You should consider finding a new job if your boss really (   ) on the terms of your contract.

D. Muir: Now to President Biden's move to approve a drilling project in Alaska, drawing criticism tonight, approving a controversial plan to allow a new $8 billion oil drilling project. Here's Matt Gutman tonight.

5 *M. Gutman:* Tonight, the Biden administration under fire after approving a controversial oil drilling project in Alaska. The Willow Project will include three drill sites with nearly 200 wells in Alaska's National Petroleum Reserve. The 23-million-acre reserve was the largest undisturbed plot of public land in the United States. [1.] _____

10 _____ for the $8 billion project, but were denied. Project developer ConocoPhillips stating that Willow is expected to generate billions of dollars for federal, state, and local governments. At its peak, it's estimated it'll produce 180,000 barrels of oil per day, they say, decreasing [2.] _____

15 _____

_____ and will add over 2,500 jobs during construction and 300 long-term jobs. Environmentalists accusing President Biden of reneging on this campaign promise.

President J. Biden: [3.] _____

20 _____. Period. Period, period, period.

M. Gutman: Over the next three decades, the project could produce nearly 240 million metric tons of net carbon dioxide. That's equivalent to more than 51 million gasoline powered cars driven for a year.

C. Goldfuss, Chief Policy Impact Officer: The oil and gas won't come online

25   **4.**_____. So, that time period is one

in which we need to be phasing down our use of fossil fuels, not

increasing them.

M. Gutman: David, the Biden administration says this is a compromise

agreement. On the one hand, **5.**_____

30   _____. On the other, they say, if they had rejected this deal,

it likely would have just been overturned in court anyway. David?

D. Muir: All right, Matt Gutman tonight. Thank you, Matt.

Notes   L. 5   **under fire** 「非難されている；批判を浴びている」

        L. 6   **The Willow Project** 「ウィロー・プロジェクト〈アラスカでの大規模な石油掘削プロジェクト〉」

        L. 7   **National Petroleum Reserve** 「国家石油保留地」

        L. 9   **undisturbed plot** 「手つかずの地区［区画］」

        L. 11   **ConocoPhillips** 「コノコフィリップス〈米国石油大手企業。テキサス州ヒューストンに本社を置く〉」

        L. 20   **Period** 「以上；（議論はこれで）もうおしまい〈掘削はこれ以上行わない〉」

        L. 22   **metric tons** 「メートルトン〈1メートルトンは1000キログラムに相当〉」

        L. 22   **net carbon dioxide** 「正味の二酸化炭素（排出量）」

        L. 24   **Chief Policy Impact Officer** 「チーフ・ポリシー・インパクト・オフィサー；首席ポリシーインパクト［政策影響］責任者〈非営利活動団体にみられる役職で，社会に対してインパクトを作り出すための戦略立案と実行を担う責任者〉」

        L. 24   **come online** 「生産する；稼働する；操業を開始する」

        L. 26   **phasing down ~** 「~を段階的に［徐々に］減らす」

        L. 30   **deal** 「取り決め；（掘削）計画」

Background of the News

　バイデン政権は，アラスカ州北部の石油・天然ガス開発計画を承認した。このウィロー・プロジェクト（The Willow Project）は，2018年，米石油大手コノコフィリップス（Conoco Phillips）が5カ所の掘削建設を含む開発計画を米内務省に申請し、2020年に前トランプ政権によって承認された。しかし，その翌年に同政権の環境影響評価に不備があることがアラスカ州連邦地方裁判所によって指摘され，承認が取り消された。その後，同社は掘削の建設を3カ所に減らす案を申請し，今回の承認に至った。本ニュースでも伝えられた通り，ウィロー・プロジェクトは1日最大で18万バレルの原油生産が見込まれ，事業規模は70～80億ドル（約9,300億～1兆600億円）といわれている。

　石油はアラスカ州の主要産業であり，2022年時点ではテキサス州，ニューメキシコ州，ノースダコタ州，コロラド州に続く，米国国内で5番目の産油州である。地元当局や多くの先住民団体は税収を期待してこの開発計画に賛成しており，環境重視の姿勢を強調しているバイデン政権と対抗姿勢を示していた。バイデン政権は，開発を承認する一方で開発の制限や規模の縮小をすることで，アラスカ州と環境保護論者たち（environmentalists）の双方の理解を得る狙いがあったが，このプロジェクトに対する環境保護団体の懸念は根強い。

▶ **After You Watch the News**　　*Exercises*

•)) **A** Listen to the news story and fill in the blanks in the text.

◎ CD2-28 [Normal]　◎ CD2-29 [Slow]

B Multiple Choice Questions: Select the best answer to each question.

1. The Alaskan drilling project
   a. will include almost 200 oil wells spread over three 23-million-acre reserves.
   b. will lessen America's dependency on foreign oil, but break one of Biden's campaign promises.
   c. will ensure that the U.S. can produce over 50 million gasoline-powered cars in just one year.

2. President Biden has been accused of reneging on his promise
    a. to never again drill for oil on public land.
    b. to discontinue most drilling projects in the U.S.
    c. to make greater efforts to stop producing carbon dioxide.

3. If carried out, the Willow Project
    a. will create thousands of construction jobs for Americans.
    b. is expected to immediately produce thousands of barrels of oil daily.
    c. will most likely generate billions of dollars for the project developer.

4. The drilling project is described as a "compromise agreement" because
    a. the Biden administration and Congress had to adjust their expectations.
    b. it will allow for an increase in the use of fossil fuels while waiting for the gas and oil to come online.
    c. it would lead to a reduction in drilling in future years and if Biden had rejected it, the court would have overturned the rejection.

•)) C Translate the following Japanese into English. Then listen to the CD and practice the conversation with your partner.   DL 39   CD2-30

A: I can't believe what President Biden has done now!

B: What did he do?

A: 1. _____

   _____.

B: But isn't that a good thing? We need oil.

A: Are you joking? Think of the environment. 2. _____

   _____.

B: 3. That may be so, but _____

   _____.

A: Yeah, but the president is reneging on a campaign promise. That's terrible!

1. 彼はアラスカの公有地での巨大な掘削プロジェクトを承認しました。

2. 何百万トンもの二酸化炭素が出るかもしれません。

3. そうかもしれませんが，アメリカの外国エネルギーへの依存は現実的な問題になっています。

•)) D Summary Practice: Fill in the blanks with suitable words beginning with the letters indicated. Then listen to the CD and check your answers.

🎧 DL 40 ⊚ CD2-31

President Biden and his (¹· **a**   ) are under (²· **f**   )
for supporting the (³· **W**   ) (⁴· **P**   ), an oil drilling project in
(⁵· **A**   ) National Petroleum (⁶· **R**   ). The (⁷· **c**   )
plan involves an $(⁸· **e**   ) (⁹· **b**   ) deal to drill three (¹⁰· **s**   ) on an
undisturbed (¹¹· **p**   ) of (¹²· **p**   ) land. The problem? (¹³· **E**   )
are accusing the president of (¹⁴· **r**   ) on his (¹⁵· **c**   )
(¹⁶· **p**   ) not to drill on (¹⁷· **f**   ) lands. Although the project
would create thousands of (¹⁸· **j**   ) and limit (¹⁹· **f**   ) drilling, it could
also spew millions of metric tons of (²⁰· **c**   ) (²¹· **d**   ) into the air.
Will this (²²· **c**   ) agreement come to pass?

E Discussion: Share your ideas and opinions with your classmates.

1. Why did President Biden decide to back the Willow drilling project? Work in a group and discuss reasons why he might have made that controversial decision.

2. This news story was aired in March, 2023. Look for updated information on the Willow Project. Has it been carried out? Why or why not?

3. How much do you know about Alaska? Do an internet search to see what you can learn about American's 49th state.

News Story
14

Air Date: March 18, 2023
Duration: 1'56"

Fury in France

The Gist ■ Why are many people in France protesting?
■ What does President Macron say about the situation?

▶ **Before You Watch the News**   *Warm-up Exercises*

•)) **A Vocabulary Check:** Choose the correct definition for each of the words below.

⬇ DL 41   ◉ CD2-32

1.	erupt	( )	a.	debt or shortage
2.	toss	( )	b.	a large pile
3.	upend	( )	c.	to affect negatively; to create a chaotic situation
4.	mound	( )	d.	to explode; to break out
5.	deficit	( )	e.	to throw

B Fill in the blanks with appropriate expressions from the Vocabulary Check above. Change the word forms where necessary.

1. Don't just ( ) your bag like that! You might hit someone.
2. Although the students expected to earn money for their trip through the pizza sale, they ended up with a ( ).
3. Mr. Jones ( ) in anger when he learned his car had been stolen.
4. What from a distance appeared to be a large dog on the side of the road turned out to be a ( ) of leaves that had fallen from a truck.
5. Our plans to travel to Guam were ( ) when the typhoon struck.

W. Johnson: Now to days of protests erupting in the streets of Paris. The unrest fueled by anger over the government's plan to raise the retirement age from 62 to 64. Protesters tossed fireworks at police as they clashed for a third straight night. Hundreds have been arrested [1.]_____ since protests began in January. ABC's Ines de la Cuetara reporting from Paris tonight.

I. de la Cuetara: Tonight, heated new protests sweeping across France. Millions hitting the streets since mid-January to protest French President Emmanuel Macron's plan to reform pensions. At least 4,000 people marching tonight in Paris, where demonstrations have turned violent. Protesters lighting fires [2.]_____ _____ and clashing with police.

C. Brice, protester: I saw a fire earlier. It's definitely pretty... pretty scary.

I. de la Cuetara: [3.]_____ _____, upending public transit, even sanitation.

You can see the streets of Paris are covered in mounds of trash. This one here really starting to smell. Garbage collectors have been on strike for 13 days now.

Still, President Macron says he has no choice but to raise the minimum retirement age from 62 to 64, arguing [4.]_____ _____ and the government risks running a deficit. The Elysee Palace wouldn't comment. But demonstrators are calling on the government to fund pensions another way,

by taxing the rich, for instance, because they say Macron's plan
could hurt blue-collar workers the most.

G. Tuffet, protester: What he wants to do is just show the markets that he can
ah... make the people—his people—bleed so he can get the last dime
from them.

I. de la Cuetara: And most of the people we've been speaking with oppose the
proposed pension changes. Meanwhile, on Monday, lawmakers will
hold a vote of no confidence in Macron's government, **5.** _____
_____. Whit?

W. Johnson: And quite a scene behind you. Ines de la Cuetara, thank you.

Notes L. 2 **unrest** 「(政治・社会的な) 混乱，騒動，騒乱」
  L. 9 **President Emmanuel Macron** 「エマニュエル・マクロン大統領〈2017年，39歳にしてフ
ランス大統領に就任した〉」
  L. 15 **public transit** 「公共交通機関」
  L. 15 **sanitation** 「公衆衛生［清掃］業務」
  L. 17 **Garbage collectors** 「ゴミ収集作業員」
  L. 22 **The Elysee Palace** 「エリゼ宮（殿）〈フランス共和国大統領官邸〉」
  L. 23 **calling on ... to ~** 「…に~するよう求めている」
  L. 27 **get the last dime from ~** 「~から一文残らずしぼり取る〈dime は 10 セント硬貨〉」
  L. 31 **vote of no confidence** 「不信任決議案の投票」

Background of the News

　年金の受給開始年齢を62歳から64歳への引き上げることを決めたフランスで，激しい反発の声が上がっている。デモ（demonstrations）やストライキ（strike）が多く行われ，野党による廃止の動きもあったが，改革法案は成立した。

　フランスでは第2次大戦後，長らく年金の受給開始年齢は65歳だった。しかし，1981年に発足したミッテラン政権が，高齢者の早期退職を促して若者の雇用を増やすことなどを目的に受給開始を60歳に引き下げた結果，年金財政の赤字（deficit）が慢性化した。その後，サルコジ政権が2010年に国民の反発に遭いながらも，受給開始年齢を62歳に引き上げた経緯がある。

　本ニュースストーリーで示されているように，フランスの年金改革は赤字が続く年金財政を均衡させることを目指しているが，改革への反発は依然として続いており，マクロン大統領（President Macron）の支持率も低水準が続いている。

▶ **After You Watch the News**　　　　*Exercises*

•)) **A** Listen to the news story and fill in the blanks in the text.

 ◉ CD2-33 [Normal]　◉ CD2-34 [Slow]

B **T/F Questions:** Mark the following sentences true (T) or false (F) according to the information in the news story.

(　　) **1.** Four thousand people have been arrested in Paris over the past three nights.

(　　) **2.** Demonstrators have been tossing fireworks and setting fires.

(　　) **3.** People are demonstrating because sanitation workers have not collected garbage for nearly two weeks.

(　　) **4.** President Macron defends raising the retirement age because the French government could run a deficit.

(　　) **5.** Many people believe that Macron's proposed reform will result in the wealthy having to pay higher taxes.

(　　) **6.** The upcoming no-confidence vote on Macron's government will probably not pass.

•)) **C** Translate the following Japanese into English. Then listen to the CD and practice the conversation with your partner. DL 42 CD2-35

A: Are you going to join the protests tonight?

B: Of course. You?

A: ¹·I was planning to, but _____

_____ .

B: Yikes!

A: It's definitely turned violent. My friend Jason was arrested last week.

B: People are angry! ²· _____

_____ .

A: You're right. ³· _____

_____ .

1. そうするつもりでしたが，昨夜，警察に向かって投げつけられた花火に当たりそうになりました。

2. マクロン大統領の計画は，私たちのようなブルーカラーの労働者を最も苦しめるでしょう。

3. 地下鉄の職員はストライキ中なので，私たちは歩かなければなりません。

•)) **D** **Summary Practice:** Fill in the blanks with suitable words beginning with the letters indicated. Then listen to the CD and check your answers.

 DL 43 CD2-36

The government of French (¹·**P**   ) Emmanuel Macron is fueling (²·**a**   ) for the proposed (³·**p**   ) to (⁴·**r**   ) the (⁵·**r**   ) age from 62 to 64. In (⁶·**P**   ), (⁷·**p**   ) are (⁸·**c**   ) with the (⁹·**p**   ) for the third night in a row. Thousands of public (¹⁰·**t**   ) and (¹¹·**s**   ) workers are also on (¹²·**s**   ). Macron claims he has no (¹³·**c**   ) but to raise the (¹⁴·**m**   ) retirement age, but demonstrators say his plan would hurt (¹⁵·**b**   )-(¹⁶·**c**   ) workers the most. Instead, many believe the government should (¹⁷·**t**   ) the (¹⁸·**r**   ) to fund pensions.

E **Discussion:** Share your ideas and opinions with your classmates.

1. What is the retirement age in Japan? Do many people want to continue working beyond that age? What kind of jobs are available to retirees? Talk to some senior citizens and ask their opinions. Share your findings with the class.

2. Many French people are angry because the government plans to raise the retirement age from 62 to 64. President Macron explained that one reason for the proposed change is that people are living longer. Why do many French people resist the idea of retiring at the age of 64? Do an internet search to see what you can learn.

3. Choose another country and find out what the retirement age and pension policies are like. Work in a group and share your findings.

 Useful Grammar from the News

地名，建物が官公庁，政府を示す

以下の例文中のエリゼ宮殿 (the Elysee Palace) は，パリ市内にある宮殿でフランス共和国大統領官邸になっており，「フランス政府」を示している。同様に，ニュースメディアの英語では，アメリカ大統領官邸のホワイトハウス (the White House)は，「アメリカ政府」を意味することが多い。

—***The Elysee Palace*** wouldn't comment. But demonstrators are calling on the government to fund pensions another way, ...

(Fury in France, P. 90 L. 22)

他に地名，建物が官公庁，政府を示す例として次のような例がある。クレムリン宮殿 (the Kremlin) は，ロシア政府官邸として使われており「ロシア政府」を意味する。米国首都のワシントンD.C. (Washington D.C.) は「アメリカ政府」になる。また，バージニア州アーリントン (Arlington) にあるペンタゴン (Pentagon) と呼ばれる建物は，「アメリカ国防総省」を示し，英国首相官邸所在地のダウニング街10番地 (No.10 Downing Street) は「イギリス政府」を意味する。

News Story
15

Air Date: February 25, 2023
Duration: 1'55"

Increased Outreach in East Palestine

The Gist
- Why are the residents of East Palestine worried?
- What is being done to help them?

▶ **Before You Watch the News**   *Warm-up Exercises*

●)) **A Vocabulary Check:** Choose the correct definition for each of the words below.

🎧 DL 44   ◎ CD2-37

1. impact   (   )   a. to increase rapidly; to soar
2. spew   (   )   b. to emit large quantities of something
3. escalate   (   )   c. to influence; to have a strong effect on
4. hazardous (   )   d. a warning; advance notification
5. heads up   (   )   e. dangerous

B Fill in the blanks with appropriate expressions from the Vocabulary Check above. Change the word forms where necessary.

1. The villagers were warned that the volcano might (   ) lava at any time.
2. Ticket prices for that group's concerts have (   ) in recent years.
3. Be sure to put away any (   ) cleaning materials before the children come to visit.
4. Are you really thinking of changing jobs, Paul? At least give me a (   ) before you tell the boss.
5. Many people were negatively (   ) by the rising gas prices last summer.

W. Johnson: We turn now to East Palestine, Ohio, where joint teams from several federal agencies are on the ground today, going door to door in the community, reaching out to residents impacted by that train derailment that spewed toxic chemicals into the air and water, where

5

1. _____

_____. Here's ABC's Phil Lipof.

P. Lipof: Late today, more than three weeks after that toxic train derailment in East Palestine, Ohio, the EPA pausing waste removal and stepping in.

10 *D. Shore, EPA Region 5 Administrator:* I'm pleased that there have been no exceedances for residential air quality standards and the **2.** _____

_____.

P. Lipof: FEMA, Health and Human Services, the EPA, and CDC all going door to door to provide information to the community. Many

15 complaining of symptoms.

Resident: I'm having respiratory problems, dry cough, ah... headaches are escalating.

E. Brockovich, activist: You're going to be told not to worry. But that's just rubbish.

20 *P. Lipof:* Environmental activist Erin Brockovich **3.** _____

_____ Friday night.

E. Brockovich: You have symptoms. You have issues. You want to be heard, but you're going to be told it's safe.

P. Lipof: The train carrying hazardous material derailed northwest of Pittsburgh February 3rd. So far, more than two million gallons of contaminated water pumped away. Some staying in Ohio, some heading to Michigan and Texas [4.] _____

_____. Contaminated soil also gathered, some sent to Michigan. Officials in both states frustrated, saying they weren't given a heads up.

Judge L. Hidalgo, Harris County, Texas: Why are these materials not being taken somewhere closer? Is there something these jurisdictions know that we don't know?

P. Lipof: Up until Friday, Norfolk Southern was solely [5.] _____

_____ created by this train derailment. Now, the EPA is telling ABC News it has instructed the rail company to immediately pause shipping waste offsite. Whit?

W. Johnson: Phil Lipof, thank you.

Notes
L. 1 **East Palestine** 「イースト・パレスティン〈米国オハイオ州北東部に位置する街〉」

L. 2 **on the ground** 「現地に出向いて」

L. 8 **EPA** 「環境保護庁〈= Environmental Protection Agency 国民の健康保護と自然環境の保護など，環境政策全般を担当する米国の行政組織〉」

L. 10 **EPA Region 5 Administrator** 「EPA 第5地域局長」

L. 11 **residential air quality standards** 「住宅地区大気環境基準」

L. 13 **FEMA** 「連邦緊急事態管理庁〈= Federal Emergency Management Agency 米国国土安全保障省の下で緊急事態に対応するため 1979 年に設立された政府機関〉」

L. 13 **Health and Human Services** 「保健福祉省〈米国民の保健福祉の向上を図ることを目的とする政府機関〉」

L. 13 **CDC** 「疾病管理予防センター〈= Centers for Disease Control and Prevention 米国厚生省管轄の保健衛生機関で，感染症対策などを行う〉」

L. 16 **dry cough** 「空咳〈痰のからまない乾いたコンコンという咳〉」

L. 18 **Erin Brockovich** 「エリン・ブロコビッチ〈米国の環境運動家。1993 年，環境汚染に悩む多数の地域住民の署名を集め，大企業を相手取って訴訟を起こし，当時，米国史上最高額となる和解金 3 億 3,300 万ドルを勝ち取った事で有名。彼女の起こした訴訟は 2000 年に映画化されている〉」

L. 19 **rubbish** 「でたらめ；たわごと」

L. 25 **Pittsburgh** 「ピッツバーグ〈ペンシルベニア州南西部の港市〉」

L. 26 **...contaminated water pumped away** 「= ...contaminated water being pumped away 汚染された水が汲み出されて；排出されて；回収されて」

L. 31 **Harris County** 「ハリス郡〈テキサス州南東部に位置する同州最大の郡〉」

L. 32 **jurisdictions** 「管轄当局」

L. 34 **Norfolk Southern** 「ノーフォーク・サザン鉄道〈米国の大手貨物鉄道会社で，米国東部および中西部地域を中心に広範な鉄道路線網を運営している。本社はバージニア州ノーフォークで 1982 年設立〉」

L. 37 **shipping waste offsite** 「廃棄物の外部［他州］への移送〈他の州などに，汚染水や汚染された土壌を移送すること〉」

:::: Background of the News

　米国で貨物列車の脱線事故（train derailment）が多く発生している。2023年4月9日付の『日経速報ニュースアーカイブ』によると，2021年に米国で発生した貨物列車事故は868件にのぼる。米国の貨物鉄道の総営業キロ数は，およそ22万2500キロメートルと日本の10倍以上あり，鉄道の老朽化や人員不足，規制の欠陥など，さまざまな原因の可能性が指摘されている。

　2023年2月3日にオハイオ州イースト・パレスティン（East Palestine）で発生した貨物列車の脱線事故により，発がん性物質の塩化ビニルなど，人体や環境に有害な化学物質（chemicals）が流出した。脱線した列車は全長約2.8キロメートル，約150両の編成であり，計38両が脱線した。事故現場周辺では川魚や家畜の大量死が確認され，住民は健康被害や不安を訴えた。

•)) **A** Listen to the news story and fill in the blanks in the text.

                                         ◉ CD2-38 [Normal] ◉ CD2-39 [Slow]

B **Multiple Choice Questions:** Select the best answer to each question.

1. The train that derailed
   a. was carrying contaminated soil.
   b. was carrying hazardous material.
   c. was carrying rubbish that spilled out.

2. Some residents of East Palestine
   a. are experiencing respiratory ailments.
   b. are frustrated that they are not getting enough information.
   c. Both *a* and *b*.

3. What has **NOT** been done in East Palestine so far?
   a. holding town hall meetings in residents' homes
   b. disposing of millions of gallons of contaminated water
   c. sending contaminated soil to other states, like Michigan

4. Which statement below describes the current situation?
   a. Erin Brockovich will be in charge of leading the new plan.
   b. Several nearby states are offering to help dispose of the toxic materials.
   c. A number of different agencies are working with the railroad company to solve the problem.

•)) **C** Translate the following Japanese into English. Then listen to the CD and practice the conversation with your partner. 🎧 DL 45 💿 CD2-40

A: How are you feeling today, Mary?

B: I've had a dry cough for a week now.

A: Oh, no! 1._____ .

B: 2._____ ?

A: 3._____

_____ .

B: Yeah, but that activist at the town hall meeting warned that we'd be told it was safe.

A: Who can we believe? I just want this nightmare to end.

B: Don't we all! This cough is making me nervous.

1. 呼吸器系の問題がますます増えているといわれています。

2. あの脱線事故と何か関係があると思いますか。

3. 環境保護局(EPA)のあの女性は，ここの外気の質は正常だと言っていました。

•)) **D** **Summary Practice:** Fill in the blanks with suitable words beginning with the letters indicated. Then listen to the CD and check your answers.

🎧 DL 46 💿 CD2-41

East Palestine, ($^{1.}$**O**   ) was the site of a train ($^{2.}$**d**   ) that ($^{3.}$**s**   ) toxic ($^{4.}$**c**   ) into the air and water. A full ($^{5.}$**t**   ) weeks after the incident, the local residents, many experiencing ($^{6.}$**r**   ) problems, are feeling ($^{7.}$**f**   ). Teams from a number of ($^{8.}$**f**   ) agencies are going door to door providing information. The EPA administrator assures them that the outdoor air quality is ($^{9.}$**n**   ) and not exceeding ($^{10.}$**s**   ), but ($^{11.}$**a**   ) Erin Brockovich warned people at a town hall meeting that what they were being told was ($^{12.}$**r**   ). Meanwhile, ($^{13.}$**t**   ) ($^{14.}$**m**   ) gallons of ($^{15.}$**c**   ) water have been pumped away to other ($^{16.}$**s**   ), where officials complain they were not given a ($^{17.}$**h**   ) ($^{18.}$**u**   ). The ($^{19.}$**r**   ) company, up until now solely ($^{20.}$**r**   ) for waste ($^{21.}$**d**   ), has been asked by the EPA to pause their efforts. The East Palestinians need answers now.

E Discussion: Share your ideas and opinions with your classmates.

1. The train derailment released toxic waste into the environment. Look for other stories involving train or ship accidents that have resulted in severe damage to the environment. Have there been any such incidents here in Japan?

2. Several different federal agencies were mentioned in this news story. Look for more information about one of the following agencies, and share your findings with your classmates.

   the EPA / FEMA / CDC / Health and Human Services

3. Do an internet search to learn more about Erin Brockovich and the work she has done as an environmental activist.

Appendix

Map of the United

States

❶〜⓭はニュースに登場した都市名で, 州名はイタリックになっています。各都市の位置は, 地図上に番号で示しています。

News Story **1**
❶ Florida Keys, *Florida*
❷ Tampa, *Florida*
❸ Chicago, *Illinois*

News Story **2**
❹ Washington D.C.

News Story **3**
❺ Charlotte, *North Carolina*

News Story **5**
❻ Callisburg, *Texas*
❼ Dallas-Fort Worth, *Texas*

News Story **7**
❽ Katy, *Texas*

News Story **8**
❾ Hinckley, *California*

News Story **9**
❺ Charlotte, *North Carolina*

News Story **10**
❿ San Francisco, *California*

News Story **11**
❸ Chicago, *Illinois*
⓫ New York, *New York*

News Story **13**
Alaska

News Story **15**
⓬ East Palestine, *Ohio*
⓭ Pittsburg, *Pennsylvania*
Michigan
Texas

TVニュース英語とは

1 アメリカ国内テレビニュース英語の特徴

　本書は直接ニューヨークで受信したテレビニュースから素材を選定し，米国ABC放送局本社からニュース映像を提供してもらいテキストに編集している。

　ニュース英語は伝えるメディア媒体の種類上，大きく分けて３種類に分類される。第１は新聞，雑誌などに代表される活字で伝えられるもの，第２にはラジオのように音声情報に頼る媒体から提供されるもの，そして第３番目はネットやテレビを介して音声情報と画像情報が同時に供給されるニュースである。ここでは，第３番目のメディア媒体であるテレビ放送におけるニュース英語の特徴を簡単にまとめてみた。ニュース英語というと使用される英語もフォーマルなイメージがあるが，実際には以下で述べるように口語的な特徴も多く見られる。ここで引用している例文は *World News Tonight* で実際使われたものばかりである。

1.1 ニュースの構成

　まず，放送スタジオにいるアンカーパーソンが，そのニュースの中心情報をリード部分で述べ，何についてのニュースであるかを視聴者に知らせる。アンカーパーソンは，ごく短くそのニュースの概要を紹介し，リポーターへとバトンタッチする。次にリポーターが現地からのリポートを，ときにはインタビューなどを交えながら詳しく報告する，というのがテレビニュースの一般的なパターンになっている。それを略図で示したのが次の図である。ひとつのニュースの放送時間は割合短く，普通1.5～3分程度である。

　●ニュースの構成

Anchor, Anchorperson

- ・LEAD
- ・INTRODUCTION（放送スタジオ）
- ・リポーターへの導入表現

Reporter

- ・MAIN BODY（現地からのリポート，インタビューなど）
- ・リポーターの結びの表現

1.2 比較的速いスピード

　発話速度は大学入学共通テストのリスニング問題で平均毎分約130語前後，英検２級では150語前後ぐらいだといわれている。しかし，生の（authentic）英語になると，かなり発話速度が速くなる。英語母語話者が話す速度は，インフォーマルな会話の場合，平均毎分210語で，速い場合は人によって230 wpm (words per minute) になる。典型的なフォーマル・スタイルの英語である，アメリカ国内のテレビニュース放送（ABC放送）を筆者が調べたところ，発話速度は平均163～198 wpm であることが分かった。生の英語でも一般的にフォーマルな話しことばほど発話速度は落ちてくるが，アメリカ国内用のテレビニュースは比較的速い方に分類される。

1.3 不完全文の多用

　テレビニュース英語では，be動詞や主語，動詞が省略された「不完全文」が多く，端的で箇条書き的な表現が好んで使われる。例えば，以下の例はABC放送で実際に使用されていた文である。これらは散列文（loose sentence）として，書きことばでは非文とされるが，テレビニュース英語ではよく現れる不完全文の一例と考えられる。

— Gloves worn by elevator operators, ticket takers and taxi drivers.

　上記を補足的に書き換えると以下のようになる。
— Gloves [were] worn by elevator operators, ticket takers and taxi drivers.

　次は，シェイクスピアが人気があることを伝えるニュースからの例である。
— Four hundred years, 20 generations and still going strong.

　これを，説明的に補足すれば，以下のようになる。
— Four hundred years [or] 20 generations [have passed since he died and he is] still going
　strong.

　新聞英語の見出しではbe動詞が省略されることはよく知られているが，テレビニュース英語では，主語・一般動詞・be 動詞・関係代名詞などを省略し，箇条書き的な文体で情報を生き生きと伝える。文法より，伝達する意味内容を重視するため，短い語句をたたみかけるように次々つなぐのである。特に，ニュースの冒頭部分で何についての報道であるか，そのトピックを告げるときにこの文体はよく用いられる。以下の（∧）は，そこに何らかの項目が省略されていることを示している。

— ∧ Sixty-nine years old, ∧ married for 35 years, ∧ lives in Honolulu.
— The weather was calm, the tide ∧ high, ...
— Today, ∧ the battle for Ohio.

このような不完全文を使うことによって，ニュースに緊張感や臨場感を持たせ，視聴者の興味を引き付けている。テレビニュースの場合は視聴者の視覚に訴える画像情報があるので，完全で説明的な文体を使用するよりは，むしろ箇条書的な不完全文の方が視聴者にアピールしやすい。

1.4 現在時制が多い

最新のニュースを伝えるというテレビニュースの即時性を考えれば，現在形や近い未来を表す表現が多いことは容易に予想される。米ABC放送のニュースにおける時制について調べたところ，現在形と現在進行形で46％を占めていることが分かった。現在形や進行形の多用は臨場感を生み出す。

— The world's largest carmakers say they **are going to** lower the frame on sport utility vehicles...
— ..., and Rome's police **are** aggressively **enforcing** the new law, ...
— Americans now **spend** more time on the job than workers in any other developed country.
— ...their budget shortfalls **are** so severe they **are going** to raise taxes.
— Now AmeriCorps **is telling** future volunteers there may be no place for them.

新聞などの書きことばにおけるニュース英語では，未来を表すのに"be expected to"，"be scheduled to"，"be to"などやや固い表現がよく使われるが，口語的なニュース英語では"will"が好んで使用される。

— In this crowd, there are damning claims that she is being starved, that she **will** suffer.
— For now, some colleges **will** ignore scores for the new writing section, ...

1.5 伝達動詞は say が多い

ニュース英語の特徴として「誰々がこう言った，何々によればこういうことである」といった構文が多く現れる。主語＋伝達動詞＋(that)節という構文では，伝達動詞はsayが圧倒的に多く用いられる。構文に変化を付けるために，主節が文中に挿入されたり，文尾に後置されたりする場合も多い。

— One result of higher temperatures, **says** the government, is more extremes in the weather, ...
— But that's the male reaction, **say** the researchers.

直接話法では，Mary said to Cathy, "I like your new car."というように，「発言者＋伝達動詞」が被伝達部に先行するのが一般的である。ニュースの英語では，このような直接話法を使って「…が～と言いました」という表現はよく見られるが，以下のように「発言者＋伝達動詞」が被伝達

部の後に出でくる場合も多い。また, 以下の冒頭例のように, 発言者が人称代名詞以外の名詞であれば, 伝達動詞が先に来る。

— "It turns out they're a lot more like people than we thought," **says** the director of the Wolong reserve.
— "I'm going to use an expression," he **says**.
— "It's strange to be here," he **says**.
— "Soon, we're planning to fly from Baghdad to Europe," he **says**.

1.6 縮約形の多用

　以下のような指示代名詞, 人称代名詞や疑問代名詞の後の be 動詞, 助動詞の縮約形 (contraction) がよく使われる：it's, that's, we'll, don't, I'm, you're, here's, they're, we're, we've, can't, won't, what's.

　縮約形はくだけた会話英語の特徴である。以下の例からも分かるように, テレビニュース英語では新聞英語とは異なって, 縮約形の使用によりインフォーマルな雰囲気が出ている。書きことばの原稿をただ読み上げるのではなくて, 視聴者にとって親しみやすい響きを与える口語的なスタイルが心がけられている。

— And the reason why, George, is **they've** learned that the Made in the USA tag carries real weight in China.
— **It's** been decades since then, but polio is still very much alive.
— Add it all up and America's happiest person **isn't** Tom Selleck, **it's** Alvin Wong.
— ..., the one that comes when you **can't** put down the Blackberry or iPhone at home, ...
— **She's** constantly juggling his needs and those of the Cincinnati ad agency she works for.

2 テレビニュースの表現

2.1 冒頭部分の特徴

　ストーリーの全体を予想させたり, ニュース内容に期待を持たせたりするために, ニュースの冒頭には短いインパクトのある表現や, やや大げさな表現が置かれる。以下の例は気球に乗って初めて世界一周に成功した人のニュースである。

— **History was made today** above the Sahara Desert－man, for the first time, has flown around the world nonstop in a balloon.

新聞英語では，冒頭の文(lead)で読者の注意をひきつけるために，書き方が工夫されることが多い。テレビニュース英語でも，新しいニュースの始まりの部分では疑問文，繰り返し，文法的に不完全な文などを用いて視聴者の興味をひきつけようとする。

— Finally this evening, *not just another pretty face.*
— *The weather, the weather, always the weather.*
— Finally, this evening, *will they turn the panda cam back on again?*

2.2 リポーター紹介の表現

アンカーパーソンがニュースの主要情報を紹介した後，リポーターにバトンタッチするときの表現である。日本語のニュースでは「では，現場の〜がリポートします」に当たる部分で，次のようにさまざまなバリエーションがある。

— And tonight, Dr. Richard Besser takes us to a remote part of the world, ...
— ABC's Abbie Boudreau is in Provo, Utah.
— It's a duel in the Capitol Hill cafeteria and Jon Karl explains.
— We asked Bianna Golodryga to find out.
— Lisa Stark explains why.
— Here's John Berman on health, wealth and birth order.
— Jim Avila is at a McDonald's in Newark, New Jersey, tonight. Jim?

アンカーパーソンが，現場のリポーターや別の放送スタジオにいるニュースキャスターを呼び出すときには，その人にファーストネームで呼びかける。呼びかけられた人は，自分の読む原稿が終了して元のアンカーパーソンに戻したいときにもまたファーストネームで呼びかける。名前の呼び合いがバトンタッチの合図にもなっている。

— *D. Sawyer*: Jim Avila is at a McDonald's in Newark, New Jersey, tonight. *Jim?*
— *J. Avila*: Well, *Diane,* in this one McDonald's alone, more than 1,000 people applied for what's likely to be four jobs.
— *J. Karl*: ..., it's probably going to last in a landfill somewhere for thousands and thousands of years. *Diane?*
— *D. Sawyer*: Okay, *Jon.* That was one sad spoon earlier.

2.3 リポーターの結びの表現

リポーターは現場からの報道の最後を決まりきった表現で結ぶ。リポーターの名前，放送局，リポート地が告げられる。それぞれの間にポーズを入れ，少しゆっくりめに言われるのが共通した特徴である。

— John Berman, ABC News, New York.
— Lisa Stark, ABC News, Washington.
— Barbara Pinto, ABC News, Chicago.
— Jeffrey Kofman, ABC News, Nairobi.

2.4 ニュースとニュースのつなぎ表現

　ひとつのニュースから別のニュースに移行するとき，何らかのシグナルがある方が視聴者としても分かりやすい。後続のニュース内容に応じたさまざまな表現を使って新しいニュースの始まりを合図している。

— ***And finally tonight,*** what makes someone the happiest person in America?
— ***Now to a story about*** the struggle between technology and family time.
— ***And finally,*** our "Person of the Week."
— ***And now, we move on to*** an incredible scene across the country today beneath the iconic symbol of corporate America, McDonald's.
— ***Tonight,*** we want to tell you about something new in the use of brain surgery to control tremors from a number of causes.

2.5 コマーシャル前のつなぎの表現

　コマーシャルの間にチャンネルを変えられないよう，次のニュースの予告をする際，以下のようにさまざまな工夫をした表現が使われる。

— And when we come back, a master class in enduring crisis from the Japanese people.
— And coming up next, what's become one of those annual rites of spring.
— When we come back here on the broadcast tonight, we switch gears and take a look at this.

2.6 番組終了時の表現

　その日のニュース番組は，挨拶や次回の予告などで終わる。

— And be sure to watch "Nightline" later on tonight. Our co-anchor Bill Weir is here—right here in Japan, as well.
— And we'll see you back here from Japan tomorrow night. Until then we hope you have a good night at home in the United States.
— And that's it from us for now.

最近のTVニュースに現れた略語

■ A

AAA   [Automobile Association of America] 全米自動車連盟

AARP   [American Association of Retired Persons] 全米退職者協会

ABA   [American Bar Association] 米国弁護士協会

ABC   [American Broadcasting Companies] ABC放送

ABC   [American-born Chinese] アメリカ生まれの中国人

ACA   [Affordable Care Act] 医療費負担適正化法

ACLU   [American Civil Liberties Union] 米国自由人権協会

ACT   [American College Test] 米大学入学学力テスト

ADHD   [attention-deficit hyperactivity disorder] 注意欠陥・多動性障害

AI   [artificial intelligence] 人工知能

AIDS   [acquired immune deficiency syndrome] 後天性免疫不全症候群

AMA   [American Medical Association] 米国医師会

ANC   [African National Congress] アフリカ民族会議

AOL   [America Online] アメリカ・オンライン：アメリカのパソコン通信大手

AP   [Associated Press] AP通信社：アメリカ最大の通信社

ASEAN   [Association of Southeast Asian Nations] アセアン；東南アジア諸国連合

ATF   [Federal Bureau of Alcohol, Tobacco and Firearms] アルコール・たばこ・火器局［米］

ATM   [automated teller (telling) machine] 現金自動預け払い機

AT&T   [American Telephone and Telegraph Corporation] 米国電話電信会社

ATV   [all-terrain vehicle] オフロードカー

■ B

BART   [Bay Area Rapid Transit] バート：サンフランシスコ市の通勤用高速鉄道

BBC   [British Broadcasting Corporation] 英国放送協会

BSA   [Boy Scouts of America] 米国ボーイ・スカウト

BYU   [Brigham Young University] ブリガム・ヤング大学

■ C

CBO   [Congressional Budget Office] 連邦議会予算局

CBS   [Columbia Broadcasting System]（米国）コロンビア放送会社

CCTV   [China Central Television] 国営中国中央テレビ

CDC   [Centers for Disease Control and Prevention] 疾病対策センター［米］

CEO   [chief executive officer] 最高経営役員

ChatGPT   [Chat Generative Pre-trained Transformer] チャットジーピーティー

CHP   [Department of California Highway Patrol] カリフォルニア・ハイウェイ・パトロール

CIA   [Central Intelligence Agency] 中央情報局［米］

CNN   [Cable News Network] シー・エヌ・エヌ

COLA [cost-of-living adjustment] 生活費調整

COO [chief operating officer] 最高執行責任者

COVID-19 [coronavirus disease 2019] 新型コロナウイルス感染症

CPSC [(U.S.) Consumer Product Safety Commission] 米消費者製品安全委員会

CT [computerized tomography] CTスキャン；コンピュータ断層撮影

■ D

DC [District of Columbia] コロンビア特別区

DHS [Department of Homeland Security] 国土安全保障省［米］

DJIA [Dow Jones Industrial Average] ダウ（ジョーンズ）工業株30種平均

DMV [Department of Motor Vehicles] 自動車局：車両登録や運転免許を扱う

DMZ [Demilitarized Zone] 非武装地帯

DNA [deoxyribonucleic acid] デオキシリボ核酸：遺伝子の本体

DNC [Democratic National Committee] 民主党全国委員会

DOD [Department of Defense] アメリカ国防総省

DOJ [Department of Justice] 司法省［米］

DPRK [Democratic People's Republic of Korea] 朝鮮民主主義人民共和国

DST [Daylight Saving Time] サマータイム；夏時間

DVD [digital versatile disc] ディーブイディー：大容量光ディスクの規格

DWI [driving while intoxicated] 酒酔い運転；酒気帯び運転

■ E

EDT [Eastern Daylight (saving) Time] 東部夏時間［米］

EEZ [exclusive economic zone] 排他的経済水域

EF-Scale [Enhanced Fujita scale] 改良（拡張）藤田スケール：竜巻の強度を表す６段階の尺度

EMS [European Monetary System] 欧州通貨制度

EPA [Environmental Protection Agency] 環境保護庁［米］

ER [emergency room] 救急処置室

ES cell [embryonic stem cell] ES細胞；胚性幹細胞：あらゆる種類の組織・臓器に分化できる細胞

EU [European Union] 欧州連合

EV [electric(al) vehicle] 電気自動車

■ F

FAA [Federal Aviation Administration] 連邦航空局［米］

FBI [Federal Bureau of Investigation] 連邦捜査局［米］

FCC [Federal Communications Commission] 連邦通信委員会［米］

FDA [Food and Drug Administration] 食品医薬品局［米］

FEMA [Federal Emergency Management Agency] 連邦緊急事態管理局［米］

FIFA [Federation of International Football Associations (Fédération Internationale de Football Association)] フィーファ；国際サッカー連盟

FRB	[Federal Reserve Bank] 連邦準備銀行［米］	
FRB	[Federal Reserve Board] 連邦準備制度理事会［米］	
FTC	[Federal Trade Commission] 連邦取引委員会［米］	
FWS	[Fish and Wildlife Service] 魚類野生生物局［米］	

■ G

G8	[the Group of Eight] 先進（主要）8カ国（首脳会議）
G-20	[the Group of Twenty (Finance Ministers and Central Bank Governors)] 主要20カ国・地域財務相・中央銀行総裁会議
GAO	[General Accounting Office] 会計検査院［米］
GDP	[gross domestic product] 国内総生産
GE	[General Electric Company] ゼネラル・エレクトリック：アメリカの大手総合電機メーカー
GM	[General Motors Corporation] ゼネラル・モーターズ社：アメリカの大手自動車メーカー
GMA	[Good Morning America] グッド・モーニング・アメリカ〈ABC放送の朝の情報・ニュース番組〉
GMT	[Greenwich Mean Time] グリニッジ標準時
GNP	[gross national product] 国民総生産
GOP	[Grand Old Party] ゴップ：アメリカ共和党の異名
GPA	[grade point average] 成績平均点（値）：グレード・ポイント・アベレージ
GPS	[global positioning system] 全地球測位システム
GPT-4	[Generative Pre-trained Transformer 4] ジーピーティー・フォー〈OpenAI社が2023年にリリースした大規模言語モデル〉

■ H

HBO	[Home Box Office] ホーム・ボックス・オフィス：アメリカ最大手のペイケーブル番組供給業者
HHS	[Department of Health and Human Services] 保健社会福祉省［米］
HIV	[human immunodeficiency virus] ヒト免疫不全ウイルス
HMO	[Health Maintenance Organization] 保健維持機構［米］
HMS	[Her (His) Majesty's Ship] 英国海軍；英国海軍艦船
HRW	[Human Rights Watch] ヒューマン・ライツ・ウォッチ
HSBC	[Hongkong and Shanghai Banking Corporation Limited] 香港上海銀行

■ I

IBM	[International Business Machines Corporation] アイ・ビー・エム
ICBM	[intercontinental ballistic missile] 大陸間弾道ミサイル
ICE	[Immigration and Customs Enforcement] 移民税関捜査局［米］
ICT	[information and communications technology] 情報通信技術
ID	[identification] 身分証明書

IDF	[Israel Defense Forces] イスラエル国防軍
IMF	[International Monetary Fund] 国際通貨基金
Inc.	[~ Incorporated] ～会社；会社組織の；有限会社
INS	[Immigration and Naturalization Service] 米国移民帰化局
IOC	[International Olympic Committee] 国際オリンピック委員会
IPCC	[Intergovernmental Panel on Climate Change] 気候変動に関する政府間パネル
IQ	[intelligence quotient] 知能指数
IRA	[Irish Republican Army] アイルランド共和軍
IRS	[Internal Revenue Service] 内国歳入庁［米］
ISIS	[Islamic State of Iraq and Syria] イスラム国
IUCN	[International Union for Conservation of Nature (and Natural Resources)] 国際自然保護連合

■ J

JCAHO	[Joint Commission on Accreditation of Healthcare Organizations] 医療施設認定合同審査会［米］
JFK	[John Fitzgerald Kennedy] ケネディー：アメリカ第35代大統領

■ L

LA	[Los Angeles] ロサンゼルス
LED	[light-emitting diode] 発光ダイオード
LGBTQ	[lesbian, gay, bisexual, transgender and queer (questioning)] 性的少数者
LLC	[limited liability company] 有限責任会社
LNG	[liquefied natural gas] 液化天然ガス

■ M

M&A	[merger and acquisition] 企業の合併・買収
MADD	[Mothers Against Drunk Driving] 酒酔い運転に反対する母親の会［米］
MERS	[Middle East Respiratory Syndrome (coronavirus)] マーズコロナウイルス
MLB	[Major League Baseball] メジャー・リーグ・ベースボール［米］
MMR	[measles-mumps-rubella vaccine] MMRワクチン：はしか，おたふく風邪，風疹の3種混合の予防接種
MRI	[magnetic resonance imaging] 磁気共鳴映像法
MVP	[most valuable player] 最高殊勲選手；最優秀選手

■ N

NAFTA	[North Atlantic Free Trade Area] ナフタ；北大西洋自由貿易地域
NASA	[National Aeronautics and Space Administration] ナサ；航空宇宙局［米］
NASCAR	[National Association for Stock Car Auto Racing] 全米自動車競争協会
NASDAQ	[National Association of Securities Dealers Automated Quotations]（証券）ナスダックシステム；相場情報システム［米］

NATO	[North Atlantic Treaty Organization] 北大西洋条約機構
NBA	[National Basketball Association] 全米バスケットボール協会
NBC	[National Broadcasting Company] NBC放送
NCAA	[National Collegiate Athletic Association] 全米大学体育協会
NCIC	[National Crime Information Center] 全米犯罪情報センター
NFL	[National Football League] ナショナル［米プロ］・フットボール・リーグ
NGO	[non-governmental organization] 非政府（間）組織；民間非営利団体
NHL	[National Hockey League] 北米プロアイスホッケー・リーグ
NHTSA	[National Highway Traffic Safety Administration] 幹線道路交通安全局［米］
NIH	[National Institutes of Health] 国立保健研究［米］
NRA	[National Rifle Association] 全米ライフル協会
NSA	[National Security Agency] 国家安全保障局［米］
NTSA	[National Technical Services Association] 全国輸送安全委員会［米］
NTSB	[National Transportation Safety Board] 国家運輸安全委員会［米］
NV	[Nevada] ネバダ州（アメリカ）
NYPD	[New York City Police Department] ニューヨーク市警察

■ O

OMB	[the Office of Management and Budget] 行政管理予算局
OPEC	[Organization of Petroleum Exporting Countries] 石油輸出国機構

■ P

PGA	[Professional Golfers' Association] プロゴルフ協会〈正式には，全米プロゴルフ協会はProfessional Golfers' Association of America（PGA of America）〉
PGD	[pre-implantation genetic diagnosis] 着床前遺伝子診断
PIN	[personal identification number] 暗証番号；個人識別番号
PLO	[Palestine Liberation Organization] パレスチナ解放機構
POW	[prisoner of war] 戦争捕虜
PPE	[Personal Protective Equipment] 個人用防護
PVC	[polyvinyl chloride] ポリ塩化ビニル

■ Q

QB	[quarterback] クォーターバック（アメリカン・フットボール）

■ R

RAF	[Royal Air Force] 英国空軍
RNC	[Republican National Committee] 共和党全国委員会
ROK	[Republic of Korea] 大韓民国
ROTC	[Reserve Officers' Training Corps] 予備役将校訓練団［米］
RV	[recreational vehicle] リクリエーション用自動車

■ S

SAM   [surface-to-air missile] 地対空ミサイル

SARS   [Severe Acute Respiratory Syndrome] 重症急性呼吸器症候群

SAT   [Scholastic Aptitude Test] 大学進学適性試験［米］

SEC   [(U.S.) Securities and Exchange Commission] 米証券取引委員会

SNS   [social networking service] エスエヌエス；ソーシャル・ネットワーキング・サービス：
　　　　インターネットを介して，友人や知人の輪を広げていくためのオンラインサービス

START   [Strategic Arms Reduction Treaty] 戦略兵器削減条約

STD   [sexually transmitted (transmissible) diseases] 性感染症

SUV   [sport-utility vehicle] スポーツ・ユーティリティ・ビークル；スポーツ汎用車

SWAT   [Special Weapons and Tactics] スワット；特別機動隊［米］

■ T

TB   [tuberculosis] 結核

TOB   [takeover bid] 株式の公開買付制度：企業の支配権を得るために，その企業の株式を
　　　　買い集めること

TPP   [Trans-Pacific Partnership] 環太平洋戦略的経済連携協定

TSA   [Transportation Security Administration] 運輸保安局［米］

■ U

UA   [United Airlines] ユナイテッド航空

UAE   [United Arab Emirates] アラブ首長国連邦

UAW   [United Automobile Workers] 全米自動車労働組合

UCLA   [University of California at Los Angeles] カリフォルニア大学ロサンゼルス校

UK   [United Kingdom (of Great Britain and Northern Ireland)] 英国；グレートブリテン
　　　　および北部アイルランド連合王国：英国の正式名

UN   [United Nations] 国際連合

UNICEF   [United Nations International Children's Emergency Fund] ユニセフ；国連児童基金
　　　　〈現在の名称はUnited Nations Children's Fund〉

USAF   [United States Air Force] 米空軍

USC   [the University of Southern California] 南カリフォルニア大学

USDA   [United States Department of Agriculture] 米農務省

USGS   [United States Geological Survey] 米国地質調査所

USMC   [United States Marine Corps] 米国海兵隊

■ V

VP   [vice-president] 副大統領；副社長；副学長

このテキストのメインページ
www.kinsei-do.co.jp/plusmedia/419

次のページの QR コードを読み取ると
直接ページにジャンプできます

オンライン映像配信サービス「plus⁺Media」について

本テキストの映像は plus⁺Media ページ（www.kinsei-do.co.jp/plusmedia）から、ストリーミング再生でご利用いただけます。手順は以下に従ってください。

ログイン

- ●ご利用には、ログインが必要です。
  サイトのログインページ（www.kinsei-do.co.jp/plusmedia/login）へ行き、plus⁺Media パスワード（次のページのシールをはがしたあとに印字されている数字とアルファベット）を入力します。

- ●パスワードは各テキストにつき1つです。
  有効期限は、<u>はじめてログインした時点から1年間</u>になります。

ログインページ

[利用方法]

次のページにある QR コード、もしくは plus⁺Media トップページ（www.kinsei-do.co.jp/plusmedia）から該当するテキストを選んで、そのテキストのメインページにジャンプしてください。

メニューページ　　　再生画面

plus+Media トップ　　　メインページ

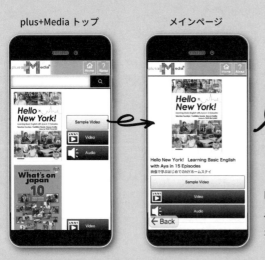

「Video」「Audio」をタッチすると、それぞれのメニューページにジャンプしますので、そこから該当する項目を選べば、ストリーミングが開始されます。

[推奨環境]

iOS (iPhone, iPad)	**OS:** iOS 12 以降 **ブラウザ:** 標準ブラウザ	Android	**OS:** Android 6 以降 **ブラウザ:** 標準ブラウザ、Chrome
PC	**OS:** Windows 7/8/8.1/10, MacOS X　**ブラウザ:** Internet Explorer 10/11, Microsoft Edge, Firefox 48以降, Chrome 53以降, Safari		

※最新の推奨環境についてはウェブサイトをご確認ください。
※上記の推奨環境を満たしている場合でも、機種によってはご利用いただけない場合もあります。また、推奨環境は技術動向等により変更される場合があります。予めご了承ください。

このシールをはがすと
plus⁺Media 利用のための
パスワードが
記載されています。

一度はがすと元に戻すことは
できませんのでご注意下さい。

◀ ここからはがして下さい

4190 ABC
NEWSROOM 2　plus⁺Media®

本書には CD（別売）があります

ABC NEWSROOM 2
映像で学ぶ ABC放送のニュース英語2

2024年 1 月20日　初版第 1 刷発行
2024年 8 月30日　初版第 3 刷発行

編著者　山　根　　　繁
　　　　Kathleen Yamane

発行者　福　岡　正　人
発行所　　株式会社　金星堂
（〒101-0051）東京都千代田区神田神保町 3-21
Tel. (03) 3263-3828（営業部）
　　(03) 3263-3997（編集部）
Fax (03) 3263-0716
https://www.kinsei-do.co.jp

編集担当　四條雪菜　　　　　　　　　Printed in Japan
印刷所・製本所／大日本印刷株式会社

本書の無断複製・複写は著作権法上での例外を除き禁じら
れています。本書を代行業者等の第三者に依頼してスキャ
ンやデジタル化することは、たとえ個人や家庭内での利用
であっても認められておりません。
落丁・乱丁本はお取り替えいたします。

ISBN978-4-7647-4190-4 C1082